Acknowledgements

Sources from which I have quoted:The Reverend George
Nelson Smith's arrival at Northport,by the late N.C.Morgan
of Northport.Stephen J.Hutchinson M.D..,for his geographical
description of Leelanau,and his "Sunset at Onomineese". My
mother,Inga S. Melkild for her trip to Onomineese.The Northport
Leader,Leroy Ellis,Editor,during the 1930's.The Leelanau
Enterprise Tribune of Leland.Stories as told bt Charles E.
Garthe,Oscar Peterson and many others.

I am most grateful to Norma (Fredrickson) Fretheim for
her contributions of stories and pictures of the Garthe Bluff's
Farm,which includes the "Log Cabin The Bluff's".Also the un-
published manuscript entitled:A Reminiscent Sketch Book -1937-
1938, by Maret Garthe,Winifred Hutchinson Schroeder,and Alice
Gill Scott of Northport.

Martin Melkild

Martin A. Melkild

and

Co-Author

Norma (Fredrickson) Fretheim

CONTENTS

CONTENTS

Leelanau Land Of Delight

In pointing out the geographical location of Leelanau to any newcomers to Michigan, it can be easily defined by placing one's left hand out holding the little finger separate from the other members; thus the "Little Finger" as it is often called becomes Leelanau County in its location with the rest of lower Michigan, with the surrounding body of waters being Lake Huron on the east, with the Straits of Mackinaw separating it from Lake Michigan on its western shores. It can be said that Leelanau is a peninsula within a peninsula!

It can be historically stated that the Grand Traverse Bay region was well known to the early Jesuit Missionaries, and reason to believe that "Grand Traverse Bay", or "Le Grand Traverse Bay" would have been so called by Father Marquette, the French Priest who first explored her shoreline.

Henry R. Schoolcraft, Commissioner of Indian Affairs, is credited with naming the counties of Michigan, some with Indian origin, some fictitious. The name "Leelanau" is also used as the name of the heroine in an Indian love story written by Henry R. Schoolcraft, entitled; "Leelanau, or the Lost Daughter", from his Algic Research of 1839. Schoolcraft is also been given credit in having given Henry Longfellow the ideas and Indian legends for his poem; "Hiawatha".

I would prefer that Schoolcraft had arrived at the name "Leelanau" from the French interpretation as its name source. Leelanau can be defined as the lee-lands of Grand Traverse Bay. Lann being the old French word or its equivalent to the English word land, singular in number. Lannou is the plural of Lan and the exact equivalent of the English word lands. Hence Leelanau - Leelands, properly speaking are the lee-lands of Grand Traverse Bay. The lands protecting the bay from the prevailing westerly winds. The body of water thus acts as a moderator to the temperature extremes of the climate, and thus explains the freedom the peninsula is afforded from frost in the early fall and in the spring of the year. This makes for congenial conditions in both animal and vegetable life, as in becoming the site for the largest cherry industry in the United States. It also excels in other fruit production, and in more recently in the production of grapes.

During former times of the geological epoch of Michigan's history, when there occured a grand glacial recession throughout the States of the Great Lakes; at which time in its movement it cut, scooped and deposited its burden in its retreat, leaving moraine hills and valleys in parallel ridges along the eastern shoreline of Lake Michigan. In Leelanau County between the clefts in the hills it left two inland lakes; Glen Lake and Lake Leelanau, the later once called Traverse Lake as well as Carp Lake. These two lakes formed by the glacier with their clear waters rank highly for their beauty with any of comparative size to be found elsewhere in the world. Lake Leelanau is fed by the head waters at Cedar Run and the cedar swamps near Cedar, where two tributaries merge to flow into the lake. The lake midway in its course is there devided -

at the narrows,at the town of Lake Leelanau (once called Provemont),both bodies of waters being similar in size. Its waters finally entering Carp River,making its way through the Town of Leland,to plunge over the dam at Fish Town,and to flow into Lake Michigan.The waters of Lake Leelanau were raised by the construction of the dam at Leland.For many years steam powered boats took passengers traveling between Fouch at the south end of South Lake Leelanau and docking in the Carp River, Leland where the Bluebird Restaurant is today. Busy tugs pulled scows laden with cord-wood,puffing and blowing clouds of steam as plodded their way to the kilns at Leland,their load of wood to be made into charcoal for the furnace which made pig iron there from iron ore mined in the Upper Peninsula Superior mines and then hauled across Lake Michigan from Escanaba.A plaque at the Leland Harbor tells of this operation.

Grand Traverse Bay offers a great asset to the Leelanau Peninsula by virtue of the fine body of water making up the twin Bays,measuring twenty eight miles in length,with the Old Mission Peninsula,eighteen miles in length devidingEast and West Grand Traverse Bay. Its fine waters are capable of handling large ships, and provide protection from westerly,north, northwesterly, and easterly winds.Thus it must have been hailed by sailors in search of shelter from storms that raged on the big waters of Lake Michigan.

From the many hills and bluffs throughout the Peninsula of Leelanau one can gaze upon its shoreline and inland with all its scenic beauty. One such point of interest must have been the tall sandy pinnacle which lies about a mile south from the Leelanau Lighthouse in Cathead Bay. It was probably a viewing point by early Indians and French Voyageurs after their Le Grand Traverse crossing by canoe from the mainland. This high pinnacle of sand has been referred to as Old Baldy,and from here one can see far down the Grand Traverse Bay to Old Mission. Down the southern coastline of Lake Michigan as far as Pryamid Point as well looking westward to the islands of the Manitou's, the Foxe's, and north to the islands of the Beaver's. It has been recorded that Major George G.Meade,Union Army Commander of the Battle of Gettysburg, had prior to the Civil War been employed as a Civil Engineer the U.S.Government, and conducted a survey party on the Leelanau Peninsula, and having used this pinnacle for his base line in the survey!

Many hardy early settlers must have extolled the virtues of the Peninsula which added to the waves of immigrants that came to settle, as they to then decided,"here we shall remain!" It is no wonder that the Indian himself looked upon this Peninsula as their paradise with its magnificent forst stands of pine,oak,elm,cedar,and maple.A peninsula provided with an abundance of game, and its waters teeming with fish. They might well have called it:"Mo-che-ne-mok-o-ming",meaning; "Their beloved hunting grounds!"

The Glen Haven Historic District

      The area around Glen Haven was an uninhabitted wilderness when Michigan entered the Union on January 26, 1837. The year before (1836), the Indians of Michigan had ceded to the United States via the Treaty of Washington a huge portion of Michigan including Leelanau Peninsula and the Manitou and Fox Islands. Indians retained the right to hunt and fish in the new territory until permanent settlers came to stake their claims. In many cases the native Americans bought back their land through monies. given them in annual payments.This of course being individual small acreages.

      Glen Haven had been used by Indian hunters and during their spring migration northwards to their summer homes, stopping on their way to gather maple syrup and making sugar. It was not known as a major Indian settlement site.

      By the mid 1850's the ever expanding people movement westward added to the ship traffic on the Great Lakes between Buffalo, New York and Chicago. These ships found the deep waters of the bay off the east coast of South Manitou a safe harbor of refuge and a good fueling stop on their way down Lake Michigan. The early steamboats consumed vast quantities of wood, and a ready labor market provided employment in the forests on these vessels routes.

      The Manitou passage by its narrowness and approximation to the vast sand dunes, bluffs so visable to passengers and navigators using it as a sighting in the passage of steam and schooner traffic on the western shores of Michigan. The attention to the 'Dunes' gave rise to the many versions of the Indian Legend of The Sleeping Bear. Some say the story originated by a great forest fire that raged out of control in Wisconsin such as that occured at Peshtigo many years ago , other versions state that a great famine occured when animals then took to the water to swim to the Michigan side . The following is an old Indian version I have been told.

      "The Legend of Sleeping Bear"

      The Ottawa and Chippewa (Ojibwa) Indians have a legend that many, many moons ago a great forest fire raged on the Wisconsin side of Lake Michigan. The fire overcame many of the wild animals that lived in the forest, while others took shelter by swiming in the great lake (Mich-i-gum). A mother bear and her two young cubs seaking shelter set out to swim for the greener shores on the other side. They first began their journey swiming with strong even strokes, but when they were about twelve miles from their goal one of the cubs was unable to swim further, and despite the urgings of the mother bear, sank beneath the waters. A short distance further, the other cub likewise disappeared.

      Mother bear(Makwa) managed to reach the mainland, where exhausted she lay down to rest, head outstretched upon her front paws, gazing back to where she had last seen her loving cubs. Suddenly upon the vast expanse of blue water there arose two beautiful islands, North and South Manitou, Created by the Great Spirit (Gitchie Manito) to commemorate a mother's undying love for her two cubs.

"Legend Of Sleeping Bear"

Upon the bluffs of shifting sand,
   Lies the legend of Sleeping Bear.
Mother bear lay atop this barren land,
   To gaze across the waters where,
Cubs and her set forth and swam,
   Seeking shelter from the forest fires there.

In fright mother bear left Wisconsin shores,
   Trailing cubs which struggling came.
In sight of Michigan,but must paddle more;
   Splashing,floundering,Oh so lame!
Onward to a safer shore,then turn to see,
   Where her loving cubs should be!

"Old mama maw-kwa,need no longer shed those tears!"
   As if in answer to her prayers,before her eyes arose,
Instead of cubs,two islands of the Manitou's did appear,
   As silent reminder from the depths below.
Mother bear in anguish need no longer fear,
   Her cubs now rest with "Gitchie Manitou".

The high wind swept spot,called the "Bear".where the Indian
legend states,mother bear her last remaining energy spent,lay
gazing ever westward where her cubs had drowned.This point has
been a beacon and landmark to many ships stearing passage between
this prominent point and the Manitou Islands.Where once these
bluffs were covered with virgin forest,but through time and wind
erosion,only a few skeleton tree trunks remanin.From the top of
these shifting sand -dunes,one can gaze down upon Glen Lake
and some of the most beautiful scenery in the world.Looking
to the north lies "Sleeping Bear Bay".It was once protected by
a long spit of land that protuded into the bay from the dunes,
creating a "Haven" within,or (Glen Haven). At one time the Coast
guard Service patrolled along these beaches,but during one
night in 1915 the entire point dropped into the bay.The sharp
bluffs that were then left,have long since disappeared,being
scoured by the persistent winds which continuously alter the
dunes area.

First White Settlers

John Lerue first came to South Manitou Island in 1847,
where he opened a trading post to trade with passing ships.He
also operated a cordwood fueling station.In 1848 Lerue moved
to the present site of Glen Arbor,becoming the first white
inhabitant on the mainland of Sleeping Bear Bay.

P.P.Smith,disembarked from the propellor ship"Saginaw"
in 1855,and became the first mail carrier between Glen Haven
and Glen Arbor area and Traverse City.

The Early Mills About Leelanau Peninsula

In 1851 by an act of the Legislature and approved on April 7th, Grand Traverse County was organized.This included the Territory previously called Omena (Omeena).

On the 1st of May 1851 Perry Hannah landed at Traverse City(site), in company with Captain Boardman whose son Horace was operating a saw mill for his father;not too successfuly though!The tract of land which now encompasses all of Traverse City was heavily covered with a beautiful stand of pine forest with only one small opening being a narrow road leading from the Mill to the dock.
Note:These new holding purchased by Perry Hannah from Captain Boardman are well documented in the "Currents of The Boardman",published in 1882 by the Grand Traverse Historical Society.M.A.Melkild,Chairman;A.V.Williams,Editor.

In June 1853 Antoine Manseau located and built the first Grist Mill at Suttons Bay.In September 1853 John I.Miller moved to Leland and erected a Saw Mill at the mouth of Carp River.About the same time John E.Fisher built a Saw Mill at Glen Arbor.Wm. Voice Sr.built the first Saw Mill at Northportin 185-.This mill was located on the Northport Creek on the west side of town. He later sold the mill to Robt.Lee.Wm. Voice then built another mill east on the creek where the M22 bridge crosses and where the old O.K.Meat Market was located,He also sold this mill to Robt. Lee in 1877.
An (Ad) run in the Leelanau Tribune in May 5th,1877, read::Mr. Robt.Lee Proprietor of the Northport Mills,Flour and Feed constantly on hand.A good supply of Hemlock and Ash lumber on hand, Also mention that the Mills were running both day and night, and that 1,400 bushels of wheat had been brought over from Beaver Island to be ground into four.
In an (Ad) published in the Leelanau Enterprise Oct.18th 1879 stated that this Mill manufactured "fork and broom handles and also made a specialty of gumming saws." In an earlier issue of the Leelanau Enterprise it states that this handle factory was operated by steam. Note: Northport had become the Center for manufacturing lumber and grain!
About this time Mr. Gill had constructed a Saw Mill as became known as Gill's Pier along with a boarding house for Mill workers and lumber jacks. In Northport he built a general store and a Post Office.He then built a barge and gave it the name"Alice M.Gill" after his daughter.He shipped lumber from the mill to Chicago and Milwaukee and bringing back supplies for his store and business. The Masters of this barge were Capt.Wm.Franklin and Capt. Robinson.Mr. Gill operated the lumber mill for twenty years,and then moved to Beaver Island where he conducted business.

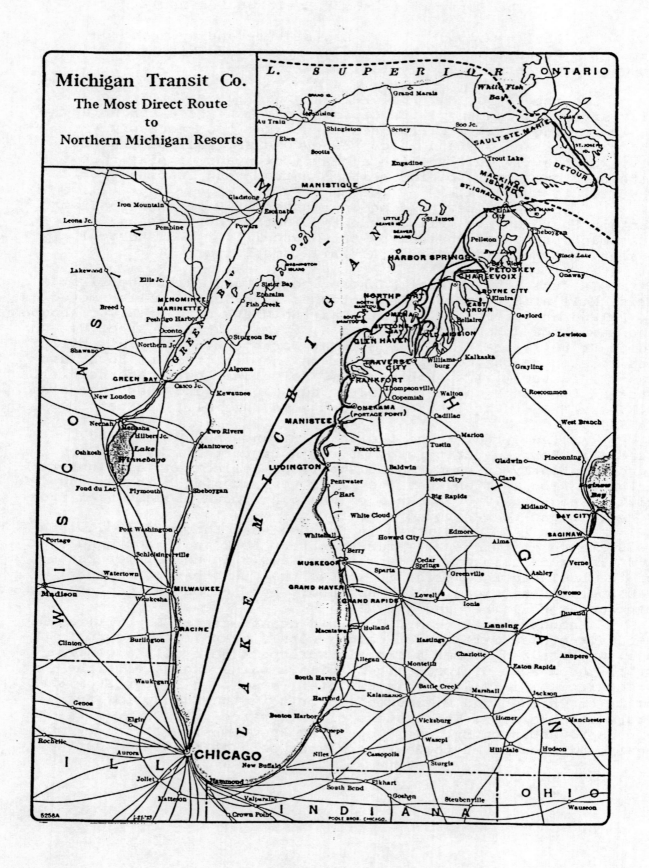

Michigan Transit Co.
The Most Direct Route
to
Northern Michigan Resorts

C.C. Mc Cartey, recognized the future potential of Glen Haven and built the Sleeping Bear House, and then renamed it 'Sleeping Bear Inn'. He first called the settlement "Sleeping Bearville", but soon adopted the name "Glen Haven". Mc Cartey constructed a sawmill near the beach in 1857, but further developement stagnated as the war between the States raged and men left to fight for the Union cause. After the surrender of the Confederacy at Appomattox Courthouse and the War had ceased northern Michigan again resumed developement, spurred by the Homestead Act of 1862.

P.P. Smith, one of the Union soldiers returning secured employment with the Northern Transit Company of Cleveland, Ohio. Smith became the foreman at the Glen Haven Cordwood station for the next twelve years. He was an organizer and a trustee for the town of Glen Arbor. He was well respected and later served as a Justice of Peace for eight years and postmaster at Glen Haven in 1880.

Mc Cartey added a flour mill in Glen Haven in 1863, but sold it in 1864, and it was moved to Burdickville. In 1865, John Helm, also a Civil War veteran, born in Canada in 1837, opened a general store in Glen Haven, but in 1867 closed it and moved to a more promising site at Burdickville. In 1865, Mc Cartey expanded his business by building a long dock out into Sleeping Bear Bay, and a new sawmill on the northwest shore of Little Glen Lake. He then purchased a tugboat with which to pull a scow and procure timber logs around Glen Lake and to pull to the mill. The logs cut into timber were then hauled overland by wagon or sled to the Glen Haven dock. In 1879 he added a ten foot wide tramway system which covered the two and one quarter miles between. For unexplainable reasons, Mc Cartey sold out his Glen Haven properties to the Northern Transit Company in 1870.

The Northern Transit Company

The Northern Transit Company had 24 vessels traveling from its company offices in Ogdensburg, New York to Chicago; and Milwaukee, Wisconsin. Philo Chamberlain, president of the N.T.C.,decided that a new agent should manage their interests at Glen Haven, including a farm owned near Glen Lake. Chamberlain chose his sister in law's younger brother- David Henry Day for the job, and a new chapter began in Glen Haven's history.

"D.H. Day's Kingdom"

"Henry" had grown up in Ogdensburg, New York, had been sent to Wisconsin where he worked for an uncle , having been promised a job on the railroad at Milton Junction, Wisc.. This turned out to be nothing more than hauling railroad freight on a hand truck. Finally through his fine education and charm he won a cashier's job inside the local offices of the American and United States Express Company, and later with the American Express Company of Milwaukee. After two years in Wisconsin, Day accepted a job from his sister's brother-in- law, Philo Chamberlain, who was head of the growing Northern Transit Company .

D.H.Day's first duties with the Northern Transit Company were in Detroit as a passenger agent, where he worked for nearly four years. At this time a first class fare from Ogdensburg to Chicago cost only $12.00. By this time Day had proved himself in business dealings and Philo Chamberlain decided to promote Day to management.

In 1878 Day was dispatched to Glen Haven to replace P.P. Smith. D.H.Day was now twenty seven years of age and he soon began losing his heart out to the Glen Haven area as well as falling in love with the beautiful daughter of the proprietor of the village hotel, William Farrant, a French Canadian. Farrant operated the frontier village Inn and rented a two-room suite to the new N.T.C.agent, Day. From the very start, Day dreamed of buying out the .N.T.C. holdings and running the Glen Haven's operations himself.

Philo Chamberlain died in 1880 , at which time ships no longer stopped at Glen Haven. The directors wanted to sell some of the company's holdings. Day scrapped together all his savings, and borrowed money from his friend Perry Hannah, as well as taking loans from family and friends to purchase these assets. In 1881 he purchased most of the N.T.C.properties in the Sleeping Bear Dunes area, including the village of Glen Haven, under the name of D.H.Day and Company. He also purchased the N.T.C.steamers Lawrence and Champlain, and set up a freight and passenger service operating from Chicago and Cheboygan called "The Northern Michigan Line". By 1885, Day no longer managed the N.T.C. sawmill on Glen Lake. He had now saved enough money to purchase it! Taking charge of the hardwood lumber business and a general store, he drew on his past experience and set about improveing and updating the facilities inorder to start turning a profit in order to repay his debts. Each day the mill cut 2,000 board feet of hardwood, and from 30,000 to 35,000 board feet of hemlock from the surrounding 5,000 acres of forest. The gamble undertaken by him soon began to pay off.

D.H.Day was a pioneer in Leelanau County's road construction, and the present road from Glen Haven to Empire was planned, supervised, and paid for by Day. Communications to Leland were improved by installing a telegraph line built by Day. He was instrumental in pressing the Federal Government in building a life-saving station on Sleeping Bear Point,which had been promised since 1870.

Eva Farrant, age 19, married D.H.Day at Empire on December 20, 1889, after a long courtship.

In 1885 Day had purchased the sawmill on the northwest shore of Little Glen Lake and modernized it with the latest equipment. This included a new tug boat to tow the logs on Glen Lake; it was named after his first-born daughter,"Alice J. Day".In 1907 Day purchased a locomotive to run on the 2 1/4 mile tramway path to the dock at Glen Haven. The locomotive came from the defunct J.O.Nessen Mill of Glen Arbor. The railway swung in an arch around the Glen Lake swamp to the foot of Glen Haven Knoll, and then to a round -house which stood behind the Sleeping Bear Inn. The new acquisition made the mill operation faster and more profitable. Workers who resided in Glen Haven could now get to the mill and the near by farm more quickly each morning, by riding the train to work at 7 a.m. and returning home at 6 p.m.. Though trips were not always without some incidents as the engine's maximum speed was 15 miles per hour. The engine had no brakes and often collided with animals who were too afraid to move off the tracks.

A crew of 15 men and a foreman operated the Day saw-mill. The smokestack for the mill was nearly 60 feet tall, so high it created its own pressure to blow smoke out of the building. The whistle which blew everyday at noontime, was powerful enough to be heard for several miles. Lumberjacks were paid 15 cents an hour and dock hands 35 cents an hour. By 1910 wages had changed very little, as lumberjacks were then paid 17.5 cents an hour and dock hands were paid 40 cents an hour. Most pay checks were in the form of coupons redeemable only at the Day store. Most all Days' employees were of Norwegian and Swedish decent. There was also a small settlement of Indians living east of the village who afforded a source of labor.

Day was a pioneer in the field of environmental conservation, as he did not believe in a wholesale devastation of the landscape, which at this time was in conflict with the philosophy of many lumberman of the times. His property, and especially in the area known as the Day Forest is the earliest known example of reforestation in Northern Michigan. These cut over lands were protected from cattle grazing and fires.It was a special pleasure for Day to watch these cut-over lands grow once again into lush forest stands of pine, hemlock,oak,ash, cherry,birch, and maple. By 1918 some of these trees were more than two feet in diameter. By 1910,Day owned over 5,000 forested acres of Leelanau County, enough to keep his company viable well into the next decade.

The trademark for most lumber-barons were huge ornate mansions and equally ostentatious lifestyles, yet the life in Glen Haven for the Day family, was comfortable, but austere in comparison. Although an imposing two-story home was built on the D.H.Day farm,(acquired from the N.T.C. Company)Mr.& Mrs. Day preferred to raise their seven children in the quarters above the store. Mrs. Eva Day was a quiet woman,intensely devoted to her children and husband.

The D.H.Day Farm, 3 miles south of Glen Haven on M-109, was known locally by its Indian name "Oswagotchie".

The 400 acre farm was improved by clearing off surrounding lands using modern equipment and agricultural methods. He had the house and barns built in the late 1880's and early 1890's. Hay and corn were the main crops grown to feed his prize herd of 200 Holstein's and 400 hogs. By the 1920's over 5,000 cherry trees thrived at Oswagotchie. Day had a foreman to manage and farm the property, and he rented the large house to the man and his family. Day's interest in the farm and his passion for physical activity led him to walking each evening from the village to the farm to check on its operation.

Day also had several large barns in Glen Haven as well, though
none of his prized cattle were kept there. One large barn in the
village housed 20 horses, 6 draft mules and nearly 100 hogs.
In 1920 lightning struck the barn and while other animals were
rescued, the hogs perished. A sickening stench hung over the
village for days. Though the structure was rebuilt, both barns
were torn down by the 1930's.

John Basch, whose relatives settled in the Port Onieda
vicinity, was the village blacksmith, who also repaired the
broken tools, logging chains, shoed the horses, and mened the
oxe yokes. He also doubled as a carpenter. Since he had neither
wife or children he lived at the Sleeping Bear Inn.

The William Day House was first occupied by Miner Farrant,
Mrs. Day's brother, who worked as the village bookkeeper.

The Warner House was built by John Tobin for the butcher
and his family by the name of Stormer. One of its last occupants
was Rosie Warner, whose late husband carried the mail from South
Manitou Island to Glen Haven. She was the seamstress for the
Sleeping Bear Point Coast Guard Station.

John Bumgardner was sawmill foreman in the early 1900's.
The Bumgardner House was also occupied by either mill or farm
workers, boarding there. The original house was a few hundred
feet to the north. John and Cynthia Bumgardner raised nine
children.

The Glen Haven School, located on the northeast corner of
the junction of M-109 and M-209, was a one- room structure which
accomodated grades one through eight. The High School was located
in Glen Arbor. The average number of children in the grade school
was 25. Male teachers were more common in the lumbering days.
Most of them rented rooms at the Sleeping Bear Inn or with Glen
Haven families who charged $20. per month for board and room out
of their salary of $40. per month. As school buses became more
prevalent, the Glen Haven Grade School closed in the 1950's and
students went to the Glen Arbor School which stood next to the
High School.

The Rude House was built during WW.I by Frank Lavance
for his mother and himself. He sold their farm which stood in
the shadow of the Sleeping Bear Dunes and moved it into the
village where he performed odd jobs for Day. His brother, Bill
Lavance, was the engineer of the locomotive and the last mill
foreman. He lived south of the Rude House in a structure which
is no longer extant. In 1924 the occupants of the Rude House were
Elmo "Pat" and Tressie Murphy. Pat, the son-in-law of Bill
Lavance, also worked for Day.

D.H.Day worked hard to promote his lumber industry in
western Michigan. He was one of the founders of the Michigan
Hardwood Lumber Association. In the 1880's he served as its
first president, and as vice president of a National organization.
At this time Michigan needed a strong, viable industry to
replace the dying lumber industry and the economic depression
of the late 1920's. Day had found a solution from his experiments
by going into the cherry growing. In 1903 the 'Oswagotchie' farm
had nurtured over 3,000 cherry and apple trees, and by the
early 1920's the total had surpassed 5,000 trees.

Tourism was also becoming a budding industry for the area,
and as early as 1910, Day had joined others in the Western

Michigan Pike Association to promote the senic beauty of
the region. The Glen Lake area came to be called "God's
Country" and Glen Lake took on the title, the "Second Most
Beautiful Lake In The World"!

The D.H.Day Lumber Company was able to stay in operation until 1923. The mill had been cutting lumber for 55
years , since 1868. Another enterprise was formulated to take
the place of the mills; the "Glen Lake Canning Company". It was
located in a 60 by 45 foot building on the village beach, in
the mid 1920's. Its construction was planned, supervised, and
financed by Day himself. D.H.Day then purchased the fruit
crops of all the orchard owners in the area at a fair market
price. The canned produce was then transported to the nearby
dock and loaded into ships bound for the large cities around
the Great Lakes. As roads improved and trucking soon outstripped
lake travel, the produce soon carried by truck, and the Day dock
like the mill, soon fell into disrepair.

Day left the canning business inthe cepable hands of
his son, David Henry Day, Jr., who had helped his father in the
lumber business. This was during the time when he had served
as the Leelanau County Road Commissioner for ten years. A new
position had been for D.H.Day Sr., n 1921 as the Michigan
Department of Conservation was created. Day inaugurated the
State's new department by donating 32 acres east of (the Haven)
to the State, to be called the "D.H.Day State Park", and thus
having the distinction of being the first State Park in Michigan history. A log cabin was built in 1923-24 on the park
camp grounds which would symbolize the new spirit of conservation. The D.H.Day State Park was joined in 1931 when the
Sleeping Bear Dunes Park was created, which then in effect,
nearly surrounded Glen Haven in a recreational district.

In 1922, D.H.Day sold a large section of land south
of the D.H.Day State PaRK AND LYING ON THE shores OF Glen
Lake to a realestate developer, and helped to devise the
the project to be called"Thr Day Forest Estates", an exclusive
summer resort .It encompassed 'Alligator Hill', an 18 hole
golf course, an air strip and a club house. Many investors
rushed to finance this prestigious project. By 1928 the Day
Forest Estate plan was shaping into reality. During this
t8me D.H.Day suffered a three months illness, and died on
April 17,1928, at the age of 76.

A 1929 announcement brochure proclaimed 'Day Forest
Estates' America's Premier Exclusive Summer Community.
Estates of varying acreage and with marvelous vistas. A
sporty 18 hole golf course, excellent tennis courts, and an
attractive clubhouse. Having ten miles of forest roads; bridle
paths; foot trails; boating and fishing.

Following the stock market crash, and as the depression
gripped the area, the econmic panic put a further developement
of the project. The golf course operated for several years
for the benefit of local citizens and tourists, but by the
early 1930's the Day Forest Estates plan was scrapped.
Investors lost all their money in the million dollar scheme.

11.

D.H.Day did not leave a will, and family members could not agree on how to divide the estate. Some structures like the store were purchased immediately by the Day children, and other parcels were sold during the depression. With the family unable to agree, Eva Day decided to place Day family holdings into the hands of a Trust Company. In 1936, Eva Day died, two weeks after suffering a stroke. On March 27, 1937, the Grand Rapids Trust Company issued an order confirming the sale of the estate under the name of D.H.Day Properties,Inc.. Glen Haven was devided among Day's children, who bought the remaining village lands and buildings at nominal fees. For the first time since the village was purchased by D.H.Day, parcels of Glen Haven became available to outside investors.

During the summer of 1934 and 1935, the Frankfort (Michigan Glider Club held meets at the Sleeping Bear Dunes State Park. A Model A Ford was operated in pulling the gliders aloft.Louis Warnes, a son-in-law of Day, and who operated the general store, started a profitable summer business by purchasing sport cars equipped with heavy duty tires in taking passengers for rides across the dunes. He hired young college students to act as chauffers.

In 1970, Congress created the Sleeping Bear National Lakeshore, which now would encompass all of Glen Haven and the sand dunes. The Sleeping Bear Inn was now closed to the public for the first time in 115 years, following the summer of 1972.
In the summer of 1982, the Midwest Regional Office of the National Park Service prepared a National Register of Histori Places nominating Glen Haven. The boundaries of "Glen Haven Village Historic District"to include the village, the tramway path, and the sawmill site at Little Glen Lake. On June 24,1983, the Keeper of the National Register accepted Glen Haven Village Historical District on the National Register of Historic Places.
Ron Cockrell, Research Historian- Park Service
With some additions, M.A.M.

The Leland Harbor

Leland

"Kitchi-mokon-o-bing"

Mitchi-molon-o-bing ,means at the river where the white
man lives,differentiating this village from that of the Indian
village located on the hill to the north,called Mich-mi-go-

bing,meaning,the place where the Indian canoes run up the river
because there was no harbor.

In 1869 a company of Detroit men organized the Leland
Lake Superior Iron Company,with a capital of $150,000.00,and
began the construction of an iton furnace,and began operating
in 1870.The furnace was built on the north side of Carp River
below the dam.It was built of brick,and stood stood ninety feet
high.It had a large frame casting house,and an equally large
stock house connecting.A flume was constructed from the dam to
furnace,the water being used to drive the the air blast for the
furnace.Six scows were built for the purpose of bringing cordwood to town from Lake Leelanau,the price paid being two dollars
a cord to the farmers who had settled around the lake,and used
in making of charcoal in the fourteen kiln's constructed in a
double row along the bank of the river,above the bridge.With
nine more kiln's built at Provemont (Lake Leelanau.Thousans of
cords of maple and beech wood were converted into charcoal and
hauled into Leland on barges,pulled by steam powered tugs.

Ore for the furnace was brought down from the Upper Peninsula in barges.Much of the limestone was procured from neighboring
farmers.The resulting 40 tons of iron produced per day was then
shipped to Detroit.

The iron furnace burned down twice during its operation
and was rebuilt each time.It was sold in 1872,with the resulting
new management operating at a profit.Through the exertion of
politacal pressure,and the promise of building a new corthouse
in Leland was voted on ,the vote by a margin of 635 to 517
against voting to move the county seet from Northport to Leland,
in 1883.This wooden court house served its perpose for many years
and has given way to a much newer more modern structure.

The year 1884 saw the beginning of the end of the iron
furnace business in Leland.The business of making charcoal iron
so far from the source of supply became unprofitabl.In that year
the property was sold to four local men who incorperated under
the name of Leland Lumber, and began operating a saw mill.

Leland's Big Bang

By 1900 the lumbering business in Leland was practically finished, and the Leland Lumber Company had gone into receivership. Wilbur Gill of Northport was appointed receiver. In lookabout for someone to tear down the large brick stack that still remained standing of the Leland Lake Superior Iron Company, he heared that John Peters had recently lost his saw mill by fire, which was located about 3 and a half miles south of Leland, on Lake Michigan near where the present day Manitou Farm Market is located. Approaching John Peters, Gill suggested that he take the job of tearing down the stack and give $175.00 as payment for the bricks. John was able to negotiate the price down to $125.00, and then agreed to take the job of dismantling the tall chimney. His problem now was to find someone willing to climb to the top of the 90 foot stack and break those bricks loose, especially as cold autumn winds were blowing off the lake. Peters went to one of the saloons where he found a former member of the Chicago Fire Department, seated at the bar, a red haired Irishman. Upon being asked about tearing down the chimney, he replied;"I will go anywhere the Devil will let me, he replied!"

A slide was erected against the tall stack upon which the bricks could be slid down. These bricks were sold and went into the construction of the old County Jail building, more recently which housed the first county museum, and also in the construction of the Star School building, five miles south of Leland.

Metal parts from the stack were hauled to Fouch where they were loaded onto railroad cars. At the very last there remained one huge cast iron wheel from the compressor. John Peters was unable to break it or handle it in one piece, and decided to use dynamite. He layed the wheel on its side and placed several sticks of dynamite in the hub,then covering the wheel with sand.

Early one Sunday morning John lit the fuse.With the resounding explosion, the villagers jumped out of their beds, wondering what had happened. They were later to exclaim; of the <u>biggest bang ever heard in Leland</u>.

Leland's Carp River origanlly bent and entered Lake Michigan farther to the north of present "Fish Town". A new break wall offers a safe harbor for many yachts which sail the Great Lakes. In one corner of the little park can be found a plaque which commemorates the old site of the Leland Lake Superior Iron Company which began operations in 1870.

Chapter II.

"THE OLD LOG CABIN"

The Melkild Family, Aunt Mary in the doorway.

My grandfather, Iver O. Melkild upon his arrival from Battenfjordsora, Norway in 1880 to Northport, puchased the log cabin that had once been the home of Peter Ringnose, who was head of the Chippewa Band of Indians that lived at Louisville (near PetersonPark). Grandfather Iver dissmantled the cabin and after moving it about a mile away rebuilt it on the forty acres he had purchased. There he settled down with grandmother Brynhild (Indergard) and their two children who were born in Norway, uncle Ole and aunt Mary. My father, Martin I. Melkild was born in the log cabin. Grandfather Iver spent most of his time working on the Car Ferry Service out of Frankfort, and it was during a crossing of Lake Michigan on June 13, 1907, that he was lost overboard. His body was never recovered. Grandmother Brynhild, died August 25, 1917, five days prior to my birth. I was therefore never to have seen any of my grandparents!

The old log cabin structure was built from hewn Cedar logs. It measured 20 ft. X 17ft. The lower section consisted of one medium size room with a narrow kitchen partitioned off in the back. Sleeping quarters were reached to an upstairs loft, by climbing up a steep ladder and then pushing up a trap door.

Aunt Mary, our spinster aunt, lived her later years in the cabin having spent much of her earlier years as a seamstress working in Chicago. I recall my sisters, Margaret and Ina, along with their friend Bernice Garthe staying overnight with aunt Mary. She would often have tea parties for the girls and would invite several of her older friends Angeline Thomas and Ida Edahal. After the girls had drank their tea, Ida would then read their fortunes from what remained in the bottom of their cups.

Aunt Mary's cabin looked so picturesque in the springtime when the lilacs and the surrounding apple orchard burst forth in bloom. Hollyhocks adorned the pathway to the privy house behind the cabin, and a large Mountain Ash tree stood near the front of the cabin, growing from amongst a pile of field stone.

I don't recall aunt Mary having any cattle or doing any farming other than putting up hay in the barn, and hiring the Abbott brothers to do this. This seemingly was quite unprofitable as the only animal was her horse named "Maude". She would hitch Maude to her light buggy and drive to town to shop.

Once when I was a youngster about eight years of age, Aunt Mary invited me to spend the night at the cabin, and of course having heard my sisters tell of fun they had I was game to try it. In the evening when it was time for me to turn in, I climbed up the steep ladder to   my sleeping quarters. After closing the trap door behind I lay down and tried to fall asleep. All kinds of thoughts raced through my mind, about the old log cabin, and I could not sleep. I recalled the stories about the ghost of Louie Kakoosh and Peter Ringnose who once lived in this cabin. I now began hearing noises coming through the cracks in the chinking between the logs, in many places where the Norwegian newspaper "The Decorah Posten" had been plastered as extra inslation. It was after midnight when I   decided I could remain no longer with all these spooks, so I crept as quietly down the ladder so as not to awaken Aunt Mary who slept on a cot in her tiny kitchen. Through the cabin door stealthily made my way, and through the dark woods I ran, which was the shortest distance to home. As I ran I heard the Hoot Owl call, and the other animals began to speak. As I ran, I began to think that bears were also follow- ing in my tracks!

The Dark Woods

Rushing through the woods at night,

    Beset with fears,in awesome fright,

Over hill and vale I ran so fast,

    To arrive breathlessly home at last.

"What my child,has got into thee?"

    Said my mother,so stern was she.

From deep within,sobs and tears did flow,

    An answer finally then arose.

"In aunt Mary's cabin I could not sleep

    I heard strange sounds from out the forest speak,

The animals from out the woods did call,

    Strange sounds I heard through the cabin walls,

So down the ladder,softly did I tread,

    I could no longer stay there in bed.

Running through the woods,I heard the Hoot Owl call,

    While thinking of Peter Ringnose,inside those walls.

And Old Kakoosh was all about,I sensed,

    That's when I collided with a barbed wire fence,

To fall disheveled with torn clothes,

    All these scratches and a bloody nose."

"It's time for to get some rest,"mother said;

    And I was oh so glad to be in my owm bed!

7

Aunt Mary and Grandmother Brynhild Melkild

Growing Up On The Farm

The Melkild farm is located a mile west of Northport on what is now called 'Melkild road'.It was formally called Peterson Park Road,to which the road leads.The farm on which my folks managed to raise six children (three girls and three boys) was only sixty acres and quite hilly.The soil of sandy loam.Dad tried carrying out a practice of general farming,relying on raising cattle and a cash crop of potatoes.He later planted an orchard of four or five acres to sour cherries which had become the most rewarding cash crop.

The folks had purchased the farm after their marriage from a German family by the name of Oberst.The Oberst's had planted the east side farm slope into apples,including many of the older varieties not found commonly today.There was the Baldwin,Winter Banana,Belmont,Golden Pippin,Ben Davis,Rhode Island Greening,New England Russet,Golden Russet,Winter Maiden Blush,Red Astrachan, Keswick Codling,Northern Spy,Dutches of Oldenburg,St. Lawrence, Seek no Further,Sweet Bough,Talman Sweet,Tompkins King,and Wagner. Amongst my favorite apples were the Sweet Bough which were planted near the front of the house,and the King and the St. Lawrence which were so mild and mellow early in the fall. We relied on our neighbors,the Rangers,to furnish us with their extra Yellow Transparent apples early in the summer from which we made early apple sauce. Several Red Astrachan trees grew up near the vegetable garden and furnished us with tart fruit while carrying out the garden chores. The Codling apple was picked and fed to the pigs to supplement the slop their usual diet.In the fall after we had harvested the apples,potatoes,carrots,and turnips,to store in the basement dad would then build a pit up in the orchard which was lined with potato tops in which we put the Ben Davis apples. These then were covered with more potato tops and dirt (an earthen mound).It was such a surprise to open this pit in the spring to find the Ben-Davis such a mellow apple.

All of these above named apples have about disappeared,but one can find them growing today at the Paul Kilcherman farm on the highway which leads to Northport Point.He has propigated over A hundred varieties of older brands of apples.It has become a favorite place to stop and to taste fruit of a by-gone era, and to be assured that these older varieties can still be enjoyed future years,

In the early days of raising apples in the Northport region a great many barrels of apples were shipped by steamer to markets in Chicago and elsewhere,but many growers could never be assured of a fair market price,having to go through a brokerage company. A great deal of cider was also was made and shipped as well.I can remember my dad putting up his two fifty gallon barrels of cider in the basement cellar.My mother(Inga) was a pious church going woman and she seemed to resent the many trips taken to the cellar by pa and his fellow works during the time of thrashing. which had turned hard by then.One year she concoted a recipe which she thought might cure the mens appetite for drinking and poured the prescription into the barrels.During the dinner break after cleaning up from thrashing the workers headed to the basement to sample dads cider.After each had enjoyed a good swig they again implored dad for seconds stating;"Martin,this is the best cider you ever made"!

In 1917 my folks had purchased there first car,a Model T Ford.This was the year in which I was born .It was fairly rare occasions to make a trip to Traverse City. I recall the rough gravel roads we traveled and especially the road leading south of Suttons Bay through the Cedar swamp. The road bed been layed out with a Cedar log base which created a corregated effect to the road bed.Along with fumes from the cars exhaust and the vibration going over the corregation I became quite car-sick and there was a need to stop the car so I could relieve myself!

In 1928 just before the Bank Holiday my folks purchased a Model 1928 Chevrolet sedan,there first completely enclosed car. The Model T Ford was then stored in the tool house upon jacks,and there it sat until one day I decided it was time to learn to drive.Following is my poem version of this timely event:

                    The Model T Ford
Pa bought a new Chevy car in '28',
        That enclosed car,to us was great.
The Model T then sat inside the shed,
        Until on day my friends,teasingly said;
"Don't you think its time you learned to drive,
        And we could run about the country side,
We could swim in Kehl's Lake.
        Come on Martin,doesn't this sound great?"
But Pa wasn't home this day to see,
        When these imploring words struck home to me!

"O K,we will take the Model T off her blocks,
        Pump some air into the tires,check for cattle stock."
Then gasoline into her tank we filled-
        Then after several hard cranks-until,
Put,put,that Model T began to run,
        Chickens cackling,boy we were having fun!

To warm her up,around the barn we sped.
                Let's head for the road,the guys then said!
The clutch had froze and there was no brake,
                When I crashed into the barnyard gate!
That old gate was quickly mended,
                A headlight was broken and a fender bended.
But learning to drive,but oh for what price,
                I knew was coming from my Pa,that night!

The guys hung all about that Model T,
                As we headed for Peterson Park,so speedily.
My better judgement was to have said NO,
                As surely to the woodshed tonight,I must go,
No supper and straight to bed.
                Later when I explained how I had fixed the gate,Pa said:
While looking deep into my eyes....
                "You sure fixed it",was his only reply!

      When I first went to Kindergarten school it was being
held in the Congregational Church as the new addition was
being completed on the school building.It would include a
gymnasium and an auditorium.I was having a great deal of
trouble with Tonsilits which effected my hearing.Dr. Flood
was the only local doctor at this time. He conducted the
operation to remove my tonsils on the kitchen table.Mother
said later that they had a hard time reviving me as I had
been administered too much chloroform.Due to this illness
I was to repeat kindergarten the second year along with
the first group to initiate the new school building.
      Until I was five or six years of age I heard Norwegian
spoken about our home until the folks it would be better to
speak English as my older sisters might develope a brogue.
      I enjoyed hearing mother read my father those stories
from the Norwegian paper published in Decora,Iowa called
the Decora Posten.I also enjoyed the cartoon strip in the
paper,entitled;"Ola Og Per"or Ole and Peter.in English.These
characters were iterant farm hands who were continually getting into trouble. Later I seemed to develope a knack for
drawing cartoons and entertained classmates in school with
drawings. I also did much art work for the "Tip Off",the
school paper .

      During the years of the depression in the late 20's
and 30's we did manage fairly well living on a farm,as we
had cattle ,horses,pigs and chickens from which we received
in turn the products of milk,meat,butter and eggs.Surplus
were taken to town to barter for staples such as coffee,tea,
flour and sugar.

      Our family attended the Bethany Lutheran Church in
Northport.I can still remember those summer Mission Fests
held each year in the Maple Grove at the Larson Farm on Johnson road. After the potluck picnic dinner the congregation

would settle down for some hym singing and preaching. It was time for us boys to sneak away to explore the woods, bluffs along the lake,and the Indian Cemetery nearby. The best part of the picnic was of course the Home Made Ice Cream.

Winter Months

During the winter months snowplows were not able to handle the secondary roads and so we had to rely on horse drawn sleds and cutters to get to town and church.Our team were called "Pete and Molly".Molly was a spirited horse but old Pete suffered from a case of the heaves.The church had a good sized lean to shed in which teams could be sheltered during the service,after providing them with hay and oats.

The tracks leading to town by the sleds soon became firm and frozen solid which made for good coasting with our sleds, and it was mostly a down hill ride to town.

In the winter our school-bus driver"Nels Fredrickson" drove a horse drawn covered sled on the route.The interior of the bus had two long benches facing each other the length of the sled.The floor was covered with oat straw and with plenty of heated bricks stored in grain sacks which kept our feet warm.Rather than ride the long route by sled bus to school I preferred to ski or sled the one mile to school.

In the winter we suffered a great deal from the cold as the only heat coming to our bedroom which I shared with my brother Oliver was the chimney which stood in the corner. We suffered from what was called frost-bite or chill-blains!

Winter was enjoyed with much skiing,sledding and hold-neighborhood parties.To prepare a good sled run meant carrying buckets of water to pack and ice the run.The run we made down the Loomis Hill across from our house crossed the road and we had to watch for teams of horse drawn sleds that might pass.After we had enjoyed as much fun sledding and cold we gathered around the pot bellied stove in our living room were we then enjoyed playing games,eating pop-corn,apples, home made candies,hot cider or hot chocolate.

The Pink Sled

In winter when the snow began to fall,
    To sled down Loomis Hill was then our call.
Our Pink sled beat all others down that hill,
    Though at times there were some nasty spills.
We carried water up to ice the path,
    Then watch to see if teams might pass....
Slam the sled down in the track....
    With icey breezes blowing through our wraps.
So cold,yet how excited were we,
    To stop among'st the apple trees.

In the winter with chores to do...
    The Pink Sled carried our wood,too!
The wood pile stood so very neat,
    Furnishing all our winters heat.
There were no plows to clear the roads,
    During winter when it snowed.
But how those icy cutter tracks would glide,
    That Pink Sled to Town,we'd slide'
Then skate upon Mill Pond when it froze,
    Till we felt a tingling in our toes.

Christmas meant a trip to find,
    And cut that Christmas tree we had in mind.
To drag it home upon our Pink Sled,
    Then to decorate it before going to bed,
With chains of colored paper,popcorn,and a star,
    Red and green candles to be seen afar.
We had no electric lights,you see,
    And only home-made things hung upon our tree.
But we were so grateful for what we had .
    For these memories I am so very glad.

Note: The Pink Sled built by my grandfather Iver has been
    Restored and is now in the Leelanau Historical Museum,
    at Leland.

The many inconveniences we had and in learning respons-
ibility which today all youngsters lack.We also carried in
buckets of water along with the daily supply of wood for the
pot bellied stood which stood in the living room and the
kitchen range.There being no inside plumbing,out only recourse
was the three holer privy on the windy knoll behind our
home. It being supplied with last years Sears Roebuck and
Montgomery Ward catalogs!!

Thrashing Time

Thrashing time was the busst time on the farm when all
farmers would trade labor along with needed teams and wagons
each day.Mr, McMacken furnished the thrashing rig.It was pulled to each site by a team of horses, one being a stallion
who still seemed capable of exciting any of the mares amongst
the other teams!With the steam run engine going at full
throttle and the belt driving the thrashing machine men were
busy throwing in the bundles of grain with the wheat or oat
straw being blown into a loft in the barn.Other men were busy
shouldering the sacks of grain to the grainery.
At noon the steam engines whistle would blow and it
was then time to line up up at an outside wash stand to
clean up before a huge meal.But first they had to sample Dads
cider in our basement.The farmers had brought their wives as
well,as they were needed in the preparation of a huge meal.
Have you ever seen a bunch of hungry thrashers eat?That is
something to be hold! The heaped dishes filled with baked
chicken and dumpling,pork chops,mashed potaoes and gravey,
other vegetables,bread and biscuits being swiftly passed
about the dinner table along with gallons of coffee Still

later they were to consume many slices of apple or cherry pie! This was something to behold,and I still think of this as aPaul Bunyan feast!!

Other Farm Chores

Trees had to be cut each year from the woods at the north end of our farm.This was a winter time job and in hauling in the logs on a horse drawn sled.My Pa had worked the lumber camps,which included the Manitou Islands.He was a good sawyer and he could wear me out with me doeing the tailing on that cross-cut saw.After the long poles were hauled in from the wood lot we would hire someone with a gas engine buzz saw to block it into suitable size and then this to be split and piled for drying and next years use.

Chores which I particularly hated during the early summer months was the picking of potatoe bugs off the many hills of potatoes.This was accomplished by flicking off the larvae and adult beatles into a pan of kerosene.

My father would call on a neighbor to help him at fall butchering time.I always hated this as cattle being butchered often had names we kids had given them,and they were our pets! I disn't mind it so much when it came time for butchering the pigs as to me they were such loathsome creatures.I did get pretty efficient at chopping heads off chickens and roosters,but their flopping and bleeding afterward did not leave me with the best of feelings.

My mother would fix us the best chicken dinners,with all the fixings, though she herself never partook of,and instead might have a pork chop.If any guests were at the table she would then tell them of her growing up in her home in Wisconsin and as a youngster having a chicken fly into her face which frightened her so.

Picking Cherries

In 1928,Emmie Loomis fro Grand Rapids purchased the Julius Brace farm which was next to our farm.This farm had been planted into Montmorency sour cherries and each year provided employment fot our family at harvest time.My older sister Margaret and I were the fastest at picking cherries next to our father. The money we made from picking cherries was used in buying our fall and winter clothes.We would order our clothes by mail from the Sears Roebuck or Montgomery catalog.Margaret and myself could strip off between ten or twelve lugs of cherries eachday,which netted us about $1.25 for a days work,being paid 12 1/2 cents per lug.

Christmas

In recalling the Christmas of my childhood,remembering how we looked forward to those days of advent,not so much as from the receiving and giving of gifts but to the church activities with presentations given about the Christmas Story.

Growing upin the depression years of the late twenties and thirties there was little extra money to be had by our parents to buy those desired gifts.Somehow they did manage to place something below the christmas tree on Christmas Eve. It might be a hand nit pair of mittens,scarf or stocking cap.

The job of finding the annual Christmas tree fell to my younger brother Oliver and myself.We took the old wooden sled which had been made by our grandfather Iver around the turn of the Century,along with an axe,we then trudged over the hill to the east where there was a cedar swamp.In this swamp we always found the right size Balsam Fir Tree.It is still my favorite tree from itssymetrical form and for its fragrant odor.After we would arrive home with it our whole family set in to decorate it with ornaments,strings of popcorn and tinsil.The Rural electrificat- ion hadn't as yet arrived,and we still depended on kerosene lamps for our lights.

John Weik,our half brother,who was our mother's first child from her first marriage and his own father dying when he but an infant.When I was five years old my brother John being twelve years older enlisted in the navy.We looked forward to letters he wrote and pictures he sent from various ports of call in the Pacific.He always managed to send us us gifts at Christmas time.

We always looked forward to other Christmas programs on Christmas Eve,as conducted in the Town Churches.These were scheduled so that we could make the rounds of them all,and thus obtain an extra box or two of mixed nuts and candy given to all children.At our church at Bethany Lutheran,the program consisted of singing the Christmas Carols,with the youngest children being called upon to recite for all the proud parents. Often times these recitals caused much embarissing moments while standing before the congregation and having forgotten ones lines and then having to be propted by ones teacher!

Then there was the usual community sing around the large Christmas tree erected near the center of the village,along with more candies to be handed out!

Christmas dinner on the farm was always a bountiful meal. Prior to Christmas had been the butchering,and the smoking of hams and bacon.At this time it was also the time to put up jars of 'head cheese and korve',a Norwegian's favorite dish which was made from liver and potatoes which was then cooked in a clothe casing.

Most every Christmas mother would prepare'Lute Fiske',
another Norwegian dish made from dried cod fish.The cod
had been caught and then it was the custom to soak them
in lye before drying.They could be then be stacked like
cord wood which they did in Norway!Anderson and Kehl and
Wrisley always carried the codfish for the Norskes. After
the cod had been soaked and cooked,it became tender and
quite palatable serving it with melted butter.

    Such were the Good Old Days,without the modern con-
veniences of today.

Left to right:Peterson Park Beach .

Inga,Margaret,Ina,Martin,Oliver,Thora,and Arthur.

The Summer Theatre

The Loomis family were from Grand Rapids and they came to spend the summer at their farm next to ours.Mrs. Loomis hired Mr. Stafford to care for the orchards.Daughter Amy had graduated from the University of Michigan where she had majored in dramatics,voice and the piano.She liked to climb up the tall hill across from our home (which we then began to call"Loomis Hill").There she would practice in throwing her voice.The sounds from atop the hill carried so well that I cared my baritone horn up there to practice,as well.My sisters didn't care for my playing indoors! This would have been around 1931 when Louis Petersen came from Ludington to organize the High School Band.

Amy Loomis was instrumental in establishing the Little Summer Theatre in the High School Auditorium.Many actors she had contacts with came to Northport to perform,some who later became quite famous actors in Holywood films.

The Little Theatre Company was forced to close in 1933 do to financial problems.Amy continued her teaching English and Dramatics and still later when she was in her fifty's she began a seventeen year career as professor of Drama and English at Vincennes University,Before her death on July 17, 1993 she had published her memoirs entitled;"Exit Laughing"!

Somehow this Little Summer Theatre had rubbed off on my older sisters Margaret and Ina.The old corn crib which had become empty during the late summer now became the spot to perform for a childrens theatre.Old bed spreads were thrown over a pole and old bushel crates became the seats for neighborhood children.The old trunks were opened of our grandparents and provided dresses and hats for the actors.The whole neighborhood becoming involved, and if my sisters could catch me I was often compelled to assist!

A Time For Fish

When Sea Gulls flew over our farm on a straight line for Northport and the fishing docks coming from Lake Michigan,I dropped what chores and ran in to town to see if I could beat the Indian women from Omena in getting some of those undersized Lake Trout that the fishermen could not sell.Other times I would go down to fish with worms off the old Car Ferry dock, which was also referred to as the Haserot Company dock.

Early in the spring us guys would have fun wadding in the Mill Creek to catch the suckers coming up to spawn.We threw them on the creek banks to the awaiting Indian women

The whistle signals

ſten when hearing the train whistle blow while coming into town I would again drop things and run in to get any arriving mail.The old steam engine was called Maude and ran on tracks of the Manistee and Northeastern.

Other times in which I made a hasty trip to town
was when I heard Lake Steamers blow their horn while
approaching dockage at Northport,discharging cargo and
passengers.Then to load apples,potatoes,etc. .I recall
the Michigan Transit steamers,the Manitou and the Puritan
being regular callers.There were other smaller Bay Boats
as well.

The Northport harbor with its many old fishing docks
became a frequent place for my friends and I to go and as
my friends,the Hagen boys,Frank and Grant were related to
the Telgards,we often hung around the Telgard Boat Shop and
were given permission to use the old dory at their boat shop.
We would row all about the harbor and docks and then plan on
the day we might have our own yatch!

Today these old docks and pilings have all been removed
and in their place is a modern day Marina constructed with
a break wall and inner dockage for yatchs,including the large
schooner the Manitou,a schooner which charters and takes
passengers out into the big lake.Where the old Haserot Canning Company Cannery once stood is now a Town Park named
after Mr. Haserot.The other marina park,in which I helped in
designing has been named the Marsten Dame Park after the man
who was associated with the Haserot Canning Company for many
years.

The Bull Moose or'Gilman D.'

Do you remember the Gilman D the tug boat built for the
Haserot Canning Company an which became known as the 'Bull
Moose'? She played an important part in transportation of the
cherry industry.She hauled lugs and returned with her hold
filled with cherries from the Old Mission dock to the cannery,
first being at Cherry Home and later moved to Northport.

The Bull Moose measured about sixty five feet in length
and around thirty feet amidship.When unloaded her bow raised
high in the bow,but a full load of cherries would ride level.

Isa Dame was her Captain and Pete Steele was her Engineer.
I remember one occasion when our School Band with our conductor
Mr. Lewis Peters from Ludington were invited to ride the Bull
Moose out to were the old cannery stood,going from Northport
and then around Northport Point to Cherry Home site of Mr.
Haserots daughters Girl Camp,Camp Caho.The occasion was to play
for the campers.In return for our concert the camp put on an
aquatic show,after which refreshments were served aboard the
Bull Moose.It was quite an outing for the band members.

Our band included many older towns people as well.Capt.
Isa Dame played the baritone horn along with myself.I understand
he used the baritone horn during times when there was a fog.
Pete Steele played the bass drum.

While on the subject of bands several of us friends started a brass qartet, they included Veryle Dechow and Grant Hagen
on trumpet,Frank Hagen on bass and myself on the baritone.Mrs.
Winifred Schroeder invited us to practice at her home on High
Street and was helpful in ordering sheet music for us.Occasion-
ly we were asked to play for the local Womens Club.We also
pl yed in a German Band which was conducted by John Schiffenider
We were called upon at times to perform about the County for
Democratic or Republican party rallies. Most all persons at
this time being Republican!

The Abbott Brothers

The Abbott farm bordered ours to the north and east. The two brothers were Archie and Robert. Their farm to the east of ours ran down hill and through a Cedar Swamp. This swamp bordered on the village dump near the Stanley Garthe farm and near-by village Cemetery. The mother of the Abbott boys, Mrs. L. A. Abbott had first owned land on South Manitou Island. Her husband was said to have been "King Strang's' printer on BeaVER Island when Strang held power over his Mormon Colony there. The Mormons were later run off the island by the other settlers and main-landers.

Mrs, Abbott had purchased this farm from Anson Braman who came from Ohio and settled the property north of the village near the Northport Cemetery. Anson had been in the Nursery business in Ohio and he again began raising apple ,pear,sour and sweet cherry trees to be planted locally. Probably these were the first the first recorded fruit trees to be planted locally, though it has been known that Indians had planted seedling apple trees at Peshawbestown long before this time. Also Reverend George N. Smith the Missionary to the Ottawa Band of Indians who settled at Northport had also planted fruit trees. Anson had also planted a hedge of Osage Orange trees which enclosed several acres to keep cattle in bounds. The only noticeable plants besides the Osage Orange trees growing at this home site today are a huge lilac bush and a purple fringe tree.

A nephew of Anson Braman, Charles E. Braman came to Northport in 1875, making his first home with his uncle. He married Alice J. Charter in 1878. He became Northport's pioneer 'Milk man'. Later this business was carried out by his Walter and grandson.

When the Maritime Heritage group in Traverse City had finished building the Schooner Ship "The Madeline", I remembered the Osage Orange trees still growing at the old Abbott property and then asking Wayne Mervau, permission to cut some in order to make dead eyes for the ships rigging, as it is about as hard

as any wood to be found!

My Aunt Mary would always hire the Abbott brothers to put up her hay. One time while I was helping them and handling the fork lift atop the hay load, and the team was in the process of pulling up. the fork with its load of hay, the first pulley with rope going through broke loose causing it to fly and clipping me on the head, I then fell to the barn floor, but luckily I recovered!

The Garthe Pond

In the spring when the Garthe Pond filled with the run-off from the surrounding hills we kids would then build rafts The pond borders onthe Northport Cemetery. In building our rafts we first collected old cedar fence posts and these were fastened them together with wire obtained from the village dump near by. We would build our fleet and then engage in a game of war by ramming each other. We propelled our crafts with a long pole.

from town had joined us for a game with our rafts,and soon
his raft had hit another he lost his footing and fell into
the pond.We then told him to hang his pants on the barbed
wire fence near by and we would dry them by building a fire
below.But the fire we built soon ignited the pants and he
was forced to return home in his under shorts!

A Northport Point Caddy

Back in the depression years of the 1930's,Northport
Point had two golf courses.The first being on the outskirts
of the Association grounds was for the guests of the Hotel
"Cedar Lodge" which then stood at the narrows of the Point
and was known as the carrying point as used by the Indians
who would portage their canoes across and into the Bay.The
other golf course on the Point was for association members
only.

During the summer to make extra money we boys would
hitch hike a ride to the Point to caddy.The going rate was
35 cents for a nine hole round,though sometimes we earned a
tip.We would average making a dollar a day.

Each golf course had its compliment of caddies with a
head caddy master in charge.We often caddied for the same
cottage owner,having proved to be especially adept at locating
the golf ball or in selecting the right club to use! There
were esveral boys ,older,and had come from the city to spend
the summer in Northport with their relatives!and caddied.
They seemed to enjoy taking advantage of us local boys.They
thought it great fun to put us through a series of tests to
make us elgible to caddy.First was the ice house where we
had to stand bare footed for a designated time.The second was
the swim test,requiring us to swim out over our heads in the
Bay,But the last remaining test I was not willing to submit
to,we would be forced to have our shirt filled with fermented
grass clippings from off the farway greens.instead I then
took off running from them,and being a good runner I soon out-
distant them .First douwn number one,then number two and three.
As I had out-distenced them considerably I now took up shelter
in a tall tree.Along they came and passing below my tree I
heard them saying how they were to give me an extra good in-
iation.Later when I reported to the caddy master of these
events the Traverse City toughs were ordered off the course.

I remember a Mr. Hawley as being favorite person to caddy
for at the Association course.Mr. Hawley had a quaint way of
following through when he swung at his golf ball.He had a six
or eight stroke handicap but was quite consistent in tournament
play.I accompanied him to courses in those tournaments to
Leland,Traverse City,and Glen Lake as his caddy.

Cedar Lodge

Northport's harbor affords one of the best and safest protection for pleasure boats on the Great Lakes. The picturesque wooded hills and jutting promontories give additional protection to boats in the inner harbor. A resort colony sprang up in 1899-1900, when Mr. Ward and Mr. Leech his brother in-law, decided to build a rustic hotel, called "Cedar Lodge". The site they selected on which to build the Hotel was on a narrow neck of land where Indians in former times had portaged their canoes across, called Carrying Point. Mr. Winans, a contractor from Kalamazoo was engaged to build the lodge. The first owner of the lodge was Mr. Fred Giddings, a Lawton Hotel man. He bought the property including the Gill farm, which then became the Association Golf Course.

Visitors to the Cedar Lodge enjoyed a delightful view of waters southward, embracing Northport three miles westward, Hearne's Point and the Indian Campgrounds to the south, and beyond seven miles to the westward looms Omena Point, earlier named "New Mission"

Cedar Lodge prospered for many years during a period when many people from the large cities came to escape the summers heat. The Lodge closed in 1947. Operators of Cedar Lodge included Mr. Giddings, Mr. Ward, Brown and Sanders, Mr. George Anderson, and Albert Wrisley.

THIS ACCOUNT HAS BEEN WRITTEN IN THE
HOPE THAT THE FUTURE GENERATIONS WILL
HAVE A CHANCE TO REMEMBER THE THINGS
OF THE PAST, THAT HAVE MADE THIS AREA
WHAT IT IS TODAY.

By - NORMA FREDRICKSON FRETHEIM
June 1, 1991
Second Edition - October 1998

Chapter III.
L O G   C A B I N

The Bluffs
Meals By Appointment

Friends and relatives came walking, others with horse and buggy and later in cars to enjoy the view and the sunsets at the Garthe Bluffs, high above the shore overlooking Lake Michigan. Garthe Bluffs Farm was located two and one-half miles west of Northport in Section 32 on the land purchased by Steiner C. Garthe in 1871.

Some came with food for picnics, but there was no shelter from wind and rain. Someone suggested, "Why not have a place to eat?" So the Log Cabin at the Bluffs was built; it was first built in the shape of a cross, three wing areas for dining and one for food preparation. Some early plans drawn say, "Park House Designed 4/29/20 C.E.G." and on the bottom "Revised as Built by C.E.G. and Erling Bruseth - July 1920." The kitchen part proved too small, so the next year a larger kitchen and living room were added on the farm side of the original building.

THE ORIGINAL LOG CABIN   1920

The Log Cabin was run by the farm family - Mrs. Steiner C. Garthe and her Sons and Daughters. Three Sons, Seth, Ludwig, and James H., and three Daughters, Gertrude, Maret and Anna, and Mrs. Seth Garthe looked after the work of the dining room and farm.

Another Daughter, Christine (Mrs. Nels Fredrickson) and two Sons, Esten and Charles were married and lived away from home but helped at times. Later, their Daughters became the main helpers.

LISABETH BAHLE GARTHE - ANNA GARTHE - CHRISTINE TALGO GARTHE - GERTRUDE GARTHE - MARET GARTHE - IN THE 1920's

Meals were served by reservation only, and much of the food was produced on the farm. Many a meal was cooked and served at the Log Cabin for the price of $1.50; later the price was upped.

The first dinner party was given by O. A. Ward of Cedar Lodge, August 11, 1920. After that, guests came from Northport Point, Omena Point, Leland Indiana Woods, Traverse City, Old MIssion, and many other places. The last party to register were guests of Mr. and Mrs. Horace P. Wheeler and were from five states.

SITTING ROOM - LOG CABIN THE BLUFFS

As you entered the sitting room, one looked in at a rustic
setting. To one's left was the desk with its birch bark hanging
lamp and Firehouse Windsor Chair, salvaged from the wreck of
the "Geo. Rogers." Here guests were encouraged to register.
On the west wall stood the old Dowry Trunk that had come from
Norway, with its hand painted Rosemaling, and the words - Gjertru
Stenner's D - Ansnefs 1834 - it usually contained hand woven
rugs that were woven by the Garthe Sisters on the hand made
loom, made by their Grand-father Bahle. These rugs were for
sale. A rocker was near, welcoming people who waited for their
table. A cozy fire burned in the free standing stone fire place
on the north. On the east wall was a round table with a hand
woven runner on it and a large arrangement of assorted flowers,
arranged by Maret. The flowers were from the garden that was
east of the cabin: Asters, Baby's Breath, Bachelor Buttons,
Calendula, Larkspur, Salpiglossis, Scabiosa, Daisies, Stocks,
Sweet William, Zinnias, Queen Anne's Lace and others, all in
a copper container.

Chairs were placed near the table. The floor was covered with a round braided rug and other woven rugs. A large stuffed snowy owl was overlooking all from its perch in the southeast corner of the room.

A small wash room was adjoining the sitting room in the northeast corner, containing a sink and a commode, later a flush toilet was added. For the help there was a little house back in the woods, - was a dark and spooky place when you went there after dark.

Behind the sitting room was the kitchen - and off to the west side was the serving room where the silverware - Community Plate - was kept in drawers under a counter, and on the west shelves were the salad plates, bread and butter plates, iced tea glasses and water glasses and tea cups and saucers. The dishes were cream colored with black and orange yellow, rather bold flowers on the edges. On the bottom were the words Staffordshire, England, or Adderleys, Made in England. A small ice box and later a refrigerator were in the northeast corner. A long woven runner rug ran the length of the floor.

THE LOG CABIN DISHES

When cleaning out the roll-top desk at the farm house
the following information was found:

FOSTER STEVENS & CO.

Hardware, Sporting Goods, Cut Glass and Silverware

June 24, 1922   Per Miss Maret Garthe   Grand Rapids, Mich.

1 Doz	8 P	Plates,	"Bungalow"	8.00	
1 Doz	6 in	"	"	5.60	
2 Doz	4 in	"	"	8.00	
2 Doz	4½ in Fruits		"	5.60	
1 Doz	Teas & Sau		"	7.00	
1 Sugar			"	1.75	35.95

July 11, 1922

3	36's Creamers	"Bungalow"	3.00	
1	36's Sugar	"	1.65	
Parcel Post & Ins. To Northport			.17	4.82

July 18, 1922

2 Sauce Boats & Stands, "Bungalow"	4.70	4.70

MONTGOMERY WARD & CO.
Chicago, Illinois

June 1923

1 Knife & Fork Set	Initial G	Adam Pattern	14.50	
1 doz. Teaspoons	"	" "	7.50	
1 doz. Soup Spoons	"	" "	15.00	
1 doz. Pastry Forks	"	" "	14.00	
2 Gravy Ladles	"	" "	5.00	

1/2 doz. Soup Spoons Queen Anne Pattern	7.50	63.50

DINING ROOM - LOG CABIN THE BLUFFS

When told your table was ready, you entered the dining room, 7 or 8 tables were there, arranged with colorful place mats of orange, yellow, green and colors that blended in well with the rustic walls and printed curtains of the same colors. A colorful centerpiece of flowers was on each table, some times Nasturtium, Zinnias, Baby's Breath, Daisys, Larkspur or whatever was out. The tables were homemade with varnished wood tops, log legs and cain seated chairs with yellow painted backs (which were purchased from Wilson's Furniture Co, of Traverse City, June 20, 1923 at $20.00 a dozen); the ceiling lights were homemade too with birch bark shades and hanging by chains. A stone fireplace graced the north wall, adorned with a clock that had been a wedding present of Mr. and Mrs. Steiner Garthe, manufactured by The E. Ingrahm & Co. Bristol, Conn., Warranted Superior and dated Oct. 8, 1878. (Steiner Christenson Garthe and Lisabeth Estensdotter Bahle were married 21 Oct. 1878.) There were also other attractive items on the fireplace.

The tables were set up with silverware, napkins, and tall glasses of ice water. The meal began with Aunt Gertrude's soup, usually pea or tomato, this was made with chicken broth, maybe some vegetable juice and a can or so of Campbell's Soup; she seasoned it up and it was always so tasty. Next came Aunt Maret's salad: a crisp layer of lettuce, thin slices of tomatoes, alternated with thin home grown cucumber and green pepper slices, topped with tiny thin slices of little onion rings; Aunt Maret wanted everything sliced thin - especially bread. This was all topped off with her homemade dressing that was put on sparingly. Sometimes she used Mrs. Albert Wrisley's Cedar Lodge Dressing, copied in the back of a cook book by Aunt Gertrude:

10 T.S. sugar	1/4 onion grated
1 T.S. mustard - dry	beat 20 minutes
1 tsp salt	1/2 cup tarragon vinegar
1 Cup oil	1 tsp celery seed

Or as an alternative - home canned peach halves and homemade cottage cheese from the farm were used.

Homemade rolls, and pickles were a must, especially the Whitney crab-apple pickles; no one has quite been able to duplicate them. And, I remember how carefully Aunt Maret put the jelly in the dishes for each table; Aunt Maret was really the only one who could dump the jelly into the serving dishes; she carefully ran a knife around the edges and we all prayed it would come out like a shimmering tower. I especially remember the Quince and its clear as glass color in a light pinkish shade; to make it one let the juice drip from a cloth bag so as to get just the clear liquid. Mother always cooked some apple with it, she said it helped it to jell.

Then the main course arrived - 1/2 or 1/4 of a chicken, depending on size. They were grown on the farms of many of the neighbors and family relatives - records show the following: Christine Fredrickson, Garthe Brothers, Esten Garthe, Elling Talgo, C. E. Garthe, Herman Waagbo, Ole Martinson, T. Roy, R. E. Nelson, Stanley Garthe, Mrs. Peter Clausen, Oscar Peterson, J. E. Brace, Henry Kelsch, John Holton, Fred Horn, T. Maresh, W. W. Thomas, Wm. Williamson, Mrs. J. D. Putnam, Mrs. A. F. Anderson, N. J. Thomas, John Southerland, Emma Egeler, Chris Nielsen, Ray Smith, Anges Thomas, Mrs. Eggert, C. I Wrisley, Wm.Bernard. The chicken were dipped in flour and salt and pepper and browned in butter to a golden color, placed in a large roaster, a little water added and then placed in the oven of the extra large wood cook stove to steam and simmer till the meat just fell off the bones! The potatoes were mashed so fluffy with gravy made from the pan drippings, usually two vegetables were served, one on the plate and one was passed from among swiss chard, green beans, buttered carrots, harvard beets, sweet corn on the cob, summer squash, all from the garden picked that day.

By special request one could get trout or white fish. Aunt Gertrude would meet the fish tugs, Nelsons, Wilsons, Stebbins, or Carlsons, as they came in, in the afternoon, and picked out the perfect fish to meet her needs. The fish was baked in the oven, with perhaps a bit of sour cream and salt and pepper over it. And occasionally a steak was requested. This was ordered special from the meat market - Chicago T-bone. The fire in the wood stove was stoked up just so with some good wood; when it was all glowing coals, the lids were removed and the steak that had been placed in a Grill Basket was put across the coals and it was grilled. All this took such care and timing. Some would want it well done, others medium and some rare and on one occasion the man said "Just pass it through the kitchen." Fixing steak was a hot job and Aunt Gertude or Aunt Anna was right on her toes to get it done just right, her face tense and perspiration beads on her forehead and her face a bright pink from the heat.

Then came the dessert, a choice of cherry or apple pie made in season - Aunt Gertrude baked the best, cherries right from the tart cherry tree with a few black sweet cherries added. Or apple spiced to perfection. And then there was cake, Christine Garthe Fredrickson's Whipped Cream Cake. She had submitted it to the "Leelanau Country Home Extension Group 1937 cookbook."

WHIPPED CREAM CAKE

1 Cup sweet cream   1/2 tsp. salt
2 eggs   2 tsp. baking powder
1 Cup sugar   1 1/2 Cup cake flour
1 tsp. vanilla

Whip cream until stiff. Drop in eggs and whip until very light. Add sugar and beat again. Add vanilla and fold in the sifted dry ingredients.

Or Anna Roy's Chocolate Cake - which it seemed only Aunt Gertrude could get light and fluffy; I think it was the quickness of assembling the ingredients.

ANNA ROY'S CHOCOLATE CAKE

Pre-heat oven to 350 degrees. (325 for glass)

Add 1 square of chocolate to 1/2 cup of boiling water. let stand.

Cream together beating well: 1 cup sugar
                                1/3 cup shortening or butter
                                1 egg yolk

Add chocolate mixture.

Fold in dry ingredients that have been sifted 3 times.
                                1 1/2 cup cake flour
                                1 teaspoon baking powder
                                1/2 teaspoon salt

Add 1/2 teaspoon vanilla

Add 1/2 cup boiling water to which 1/2 teaspoon soda has been added.

Pour into an 8 in. X 8 in. square pan and bake for 25 to 30 minutes till tests done.

This chocolate cake was frosted with a seven minute frosting. Aunt Gertrude here again was the expert; she cooked the sugar and water till it spun a thread and then was slowly added to the egg white that was beaten over hot water till it stood in perfect peaks, and when it cooled on the cake had just a thin crust over it. All the desserts were served with home-made ice cream. Aunt Gertrude would make the custard and the brothers from the farm would come and start the gas engine - or later used the tractor and long belt and hooked up to the large 10 gallon ice cream freezer and froze the ice cream; what a mouth watering treat it was to lick the hugh dasher. The ice cream was then packed in canisters and placed in the large green ice chest in the room back of the kitchen. The ice from the chest had been cut perhaps from Kehl's Lake or the Bay the winter before and put in the ice house at the farm. All of this good food was accompanied by good coffee, hot or iced tea and milk, whatever hit your fancy.

There were times when things just didn't go as smoothly as everyone wanted. We won't dwell too much on Aunt Gertrude spilling the Harvard beet juice all down her front, looked like blood -- or the time she just disappeared during the serving of a busy evening, and later was found lying on the ground behind the cabin; she had come down with the stomach flu and was so ill, "I couldn't have dished up, even if it were the President," she said. Or the time when she stooped down by the oven and lost her hold on the big roaster full of chicken and the hot gravy spilled out -- but thanks to her big full rayon under bloomers she wasn't burned.

Then there were the evenings when the cabin was full of guests and it started to rain hard and James H. decided it was the perfect time to drag the road to get out the bumps -- needless to say the guests had a time to drive over the muddy, slippery road through the orchard to get home, some times sliding off into the orchard.

THE LOG CABIN THE BLUFFS

Each fall the Log Cabin was turned over to the Bethany Lutheran Church Women, and with the help of the Garthe Sisters a Smorgasboard was held. The sitting room was set up with a long table, usually tiered. All the goodies of their Norwegian heritage were placed on it. I remember Aunt Gertrude cooking away, making her Head Cheese, baking Spritz, Krumkaka and Fattigmand. Mother made Rommegrot. Mrs. Clausen made Norwegian Fish Balls. And there were also all the other goodies that went with it.

In the column "Food Ideas" copyright 1938, written by Edith M. Barber, she says quote "The editor of this column has been doing a bit of traveling recently. It was not such a very long trip. Most of it was in New York state and Michigan.......One of the most interesting meals of our trip was a Norwegian supper which was the closing event of the season at the Garthe Log Cabin on the Northport peninsula. As this was prepared and served by the members of the Lutheran church, many of whom are of Norwegian descent, we had an authentic Scandinavian meal. There were huge platters of Appetizers and canapes, after which came meat balls, boiled potatoes, of course, plenty of coffee and several kinds of special cheese and salad. For Dessert there were trays of Norwegian pastries and cakes of special varieties. We went on our way the next morning, laden with fruit, among which was a special Norwegian apple developed and grown on the Garthe farm."

This Smorgasboard ended the season for another summer at the Log Cabin.

There were many who helped over the years, waitresses to name some - Norma Garthe Karkau, Anna Roy Winowiski, Esther Garthe Guptill, Randa Fredrickson, Elizabeth Garthe Melkild, Katherine Garthe Winchell, Christine Talgo Garthe, Christine Garthe Fredrickson, Elaine Southwell Fredrickson, and even Eugene Massilink who later became Frank Lloyd Wright's Secretary and myself.

Gertrude Waagbo Lee was a great help with her dish washing. Gertrude Garthe was the chief cook. Maret Garthe was the gardener (with help from others), flower arranger, salad maker, hostess and all around tidy upper. Anna Garthe cleaned and got the vegetables and chicken ready for cooking.

It wasn't all work and no play -- the waitresses always tried to work in a trip to the beach, down the trail and have a swim each afternoon. I only helped out evenings when the farm work was done, and one nice day Katherine wrote a poem,

TO NORMA ON HAYING

Between the edges mow on mow The sturdy weeds and grasses grow
And far below the crickets cry While hot old Sol Travels the
                                                         sky
O hot and dusty task thou art! To swim - or hay - how far apart
These pastimes are -- The sloping field - the sandy shore!
But only once a year the task Of mowing hay is here; I ask
That when with haying you are through You come. We'll float
                                              in water blue.

The last ones to run the cabin were Anna Garthe and Randa
Fredrickson. The cabin closed for business August 31, 1953.
It closed for a number of reasons, government rules, a lack
of help (the original Garthe family were getting older), and
financial costs of meeting the new health standards and rules.
After it was closed it was rented out as a family dwelling.
Then in 1990 it was sold to a private party and is no longer
in the ownership of the Garthe family.

    But let us not forget the history of the Log Cabin at The
Bluffs. For it was here that so many came to enjoy by the
Bluffs, that overlooked Lake Michigan, the beautiful sunsets
and eat the wonderful food that was served by the Garthe family.

THE GARTHE SISTERS
MARET - ANNA - GERTRUDE - CHRISTINE

After looking through the three register books of the Log Cabin and then finding some ledgers with accounts in, I thought it would be fun to see if I could come up with a number for meals cooked and served. I soon found out some signed, "and party" and some signed "and family;" there were pages that were hard to read and I'm sure some didn't sign at all. There were some figures down for the exact number for some years, these figures have an asterisk (*) behind them. Therefore this isn't an exact count -- but draw your own conclusions about the number of meals cooked and served. I also looked at the places they came from and found out that all of the present 50 states were accounted for with the exception of - Delaware, Montana, Utah, Vermont and Wyoming. There were also people from the following countries: Germany, England, Denmark, Canada, Turkey, France, Czechoslovakia, China, Australia, Austria, Norway, Russia, Italy, Scotland, Japan, Buenos Aires, Argentina, South America, New Zealand, Johannesburg, South Africa, Singapore.

YEAR	OPENING DATE AS REGISTERED	CLOSING DATE AS REGISTERED	NUMBER REGISTERED
1920	August 11	September 11	241
1921	June 19	September 25	454
1922	June 20	September 6	601
1923	June 27	September 29	789
1924	June 9	September 24	1926*
1925	June 12	September 19	758
1926	May 23	August 22	2311*
1927	July 13	September 18	1581*
1928	July 11	September 22	2223*
1929	July 9	September 15	2041*
1930	June 19	September 15	2219*
1931	May 30	September 20	1911*
1932	May 29	September 25	1470*
1933	May 27	September 11	1528*
1934	May 30	September 16	1800*
1935	May 30	September 11	1443*
1936	June 7	September 26	1189*
1937	May 29	September 13	1310*
1938	May 28	September 4	1195*
1939	May 27	October 1	1665*
1940	May 30	September 7	1234*
1941	May 30	September 10	1245*
1942	July 1	September 2	1070*
1943	June 29	August 28	1003*
1944	June 26	September 4	228
1945	June 4	September 3	283
1946	July 1	October 12	428
1947	July 1	August 13	289
1948	July 8	August 30	417

YEAR	OPENING DATE AS REGISTERED	CLOSING DATE AS REGISTERED	NUMBER REGISTERED
1949	July 3	August 30	433
1950	July 2	August 31	323
1951	July 1	August 31	440
1952	July 1	August 30	480
1953	July 2	August 31	520
34 years			37,048

BUILDING THE LOG CABIN

1920

May		L. R. Sogge - Cement	$ 15.00
June	5	Kehl & Wrisley - nails	2.48
	11	Potatoes Growers - SB - Cement	26.50
July	13	A. H. Milliken - freight on 4 rolls roofing	.71
	15	A. H. Milliken - 150 bricks & 25# fine clay	4.28
	8	Kehl & Wrisley - nails	1.05
	8	D. H. Scott - nails	1.75
	13	D. H. Scott - nails	1.10
	13	Kehl & Wrisley - nails	1.40
	31	Walter Barth - 1800 ft. lumber	79.29
Aug.	9	Kehl & Wrisley - tacks	.20
	4	Kehl & Wrisley - nails and hardware	9.03
	5	Joe Gagnon, mason work - fire place	25.75
	9	Hannah Lay & Co. - brick & clay	9.25
	19	Elling Bruseth - labor	90.00
	20	A. F. Anderson & Co.	68.00
			$ 335.79

1921

Mar.	26	Farm Bureau - screws	.35
	26	Leslie - 25 logs at 65¢	16.25
Apr.	14	Leslie - logs	4.00
	23	Kehl & Wrisley - nails	.70
	30	A. H. Milliken - freight on flues	2.68
	26	Hannah Lay & Co. - Tile & Bricks (100 fire bricks)	17.90
May	7	Kehl & Wrisley - nails and hammer handle	1.15
	14	Kehl & Wrisley	.50
	1	Peter Bahle - labor	15.00
	10	Carl Garthe - labor	25.00
	11	Peterson - SB - lumber 1050'	42.75
	21	Carl Garthe - labor	37.00
June	6	L. R. Sogge - asbestos and pipe	1.00
	6	Kehl & Wrisley - stove pipe	2.35
July	7	Carl Garthe - 25 windows	32.50
	14	Leslie - balance on poles	3.00
Aug.	6	Sears Roebuck & Co. lantern	7.06
Nov.	12	Telephone Co. putting in phone in cabin and swamp	25.79
Dec.	16	Kehl & Wrisley - windows and nails etc.	20.10
			$ 255.08

1922

Jan.		Kehl & Wrisley - Merc. & Windows	$ 24.80
	13	Kehl & Wrisley - hinges and screws	2.65
	20	Kehl & Wrisley - linseed oil	6.25
Apr.	28	Montgormery Ward - 4 sheets zinc	8.40
	28	Sears Roebuck - 25 gal stain	28.50
May	3	Expenses on zinc	1.75
	27	R. E. Mervau - paint	7.00
	30	Freight on stain	1.93
Jun.	17	Kehl & Wrisley - paint	.35
	15	Sears Roebuck - oil cloth	4.48
	21	Sogge's - ice cream freezer	9.00
	21	Asa Ostrander - valve	1.50
	24	Sears Roebuck - oil cloth 12 yards	4.36
May	18	Kehl & Wrisley - perculator coffee	4.00
	22	Kehl & Wrisley - 2 paint brushes	.80
	23	Kehl & Wrisley - 4 gal. linseed oil	6.00
Jun.	17	Kehl & Wrisley - paint	1.10
Aug.	1	Kehl & Wrisley - 2 panes of glass	.50
			$ 113.37

In 1922 the lighting plant and fixtures were
    put in at the farm and the Log Cabin - $ 614.17
    1923 expenses on motor, bulbs, Chris Nielson,
    and the company that things were bought
    from   187.06
    1924 Jun. 14   light bulbs   11.42
                                                $ 812.65

1924

May	3	A. H. Milliken - freight on tile	$ 6.16
	2	Stoddard Dick & Co. - 101 pieces tile for cooler	10.02
	6	W. C. Liebler - to apply on ice cream freezer	20.00
	29	Sogge Bros - cement for cooler	14.50
	8	A. F. Anderson & Co. - paint for chairs	4.00
Jun.	18	Kehl & Wrisley - 3 windows, paint, putty	5.20
	20	Kehl & Wrisley - paint	1.10
	21	Albert Pick & Co. - hardward	14.15
	30	John Sanborn - freight on above	3.60
	23	Kehl & Wrisley - turpentine	.25
	30	Creamery - 2 tubs and cans for ice cream freezer	17.82
Aug.	1	W. C. Liebler - Balance on Freezer	22.10
	9	Armstrong Cork Insulation Co. - cork for cooler	33.30
	15	C. H. Chadsey - Windows & Doors	41.00
			$ 193.20

My dear Garthe Family;

        I have intended to write for so long.I enjoyed both
Christine's and Mary's letters so very much-and the lovely
photographs of the log cabin.But this has been the fullest
busiest,and most exciting winter in my life,and somehow letter
writing has had to be completely overshadowed   by work-
and workin so many different directions as to almost confusing
Besides doing a good deal of painting this winter ,I have been
working on model houses,hauling wood for the fires,and earni
my keep by being "corresponding secretary" for the organ-
ization.And it seems although I bet Ann won't believeit,I make
better secretary then I look or act.ButI have time to paint
and time to sing.Incidently I have done a great deal of singin
this winter.Every Sunday evening prominent people come to
Taliesin from Madison and Milwaukee and Chicago and we give
musical programs. I have learned a repetoire of Beeethoven,
Brahms,Schumann,Foure,and Debussy. People seem to enjoy hearir
me sing and because of much singing my voice is developing.

        The privilege of being here is great. The winter has
been a hard one because Mr. Wrght has extremely limited funds
with which to work.There are no endowments and money comes in
too slowly. It has been hard to get wood.Besides two boilers
there are twenty fireplaces to feed and the weather has been
twenty below several times during the winter- so you see we
have dug great holes in the forest.

        The lack of substantial money here is a great crime.Th
endeavor is a tremendous one. Mr Wright is undoubtedly the
greatest individual in the art field today. But for his
gigantic nerve and vigor and belief in an ideal he would be ir
the same position with thousands and thousands of others
today. With his beliefs,however,he transcends all others.If
there were ever a "spiritual awakening" apparent-there is one
here. We work hard all week-getting up at6:30 for breakfast
and on Sunday morning we go walking across the valley to the
little Unitarian Chapel built by Mr. Wright's Welsh fore-
fathers,the Loyd Jones.Here we have listened to ministers fro
Madison and Chicago who come to spend the day-Unitarians,all
Protestant denominations,Catholic priests,Jewish Rabbis-and
even occasionally philosephers from different colloges.All
great faiths-at the top-being one faith.

        It is the idealist life essentially.But the cold win
from the north is real enough.Incidentally have gained ten
pounds,and have not been sick once during the entire winter.
would be impossible for me to give you an adequate picture of
life here.I am sendinga prospectus of the fellowship-it may
give you an inkling of what is happening.

How have you enjoyed the winter? Better still-the SPRING? There is no evidence of spring here than the warm sun and south wind and a faint touch of green on the hills,and suppose Northport sees no more.But I hear rumors from further south that the lilacsand apple blossoms on the way.

Then the cabin will begin to burst-with with buds, won't it?I hope sometime this summer I can drive up to Northport,but the work here is facinating and in summer still more to do(building),and I may have to be forgiven for staying throughout the summer.
Do you hear from Esther Garthe?

My mother writes that Amy Loomis is having a "spring season" of plays in Grand Rapids.Her first play was Autum Crocus-remember it?But mother didn't like it at all and is afraid that the company will fail again.Amy has almost too much nerve,I think. I wonder if she will nturn to Northport. Somehow it strikes me as being a kind of futile thing to do-the tremendous work to assemble these plays-and then the agony to make up the deficits-all for what?

Margaret and Martin Melkild have been sending me drawings during the winter. I have enjoyed seeing them tremendously and encourage them to draw more.Margaret, especially,has been doing really good work.

Ernest Brooks is a composer here and has arranged a new setting for "Bendemeer's Stream"It is really very nice-the same melody with new accompainment and I want to sing it. But Ernest has only the words for the first verse.Could you send me your copy of it for a short timeif you are not using it and then we can get the words and the melody correct and I'll sing it for you!Thank youfor doing this immensely!

I hear that Reverend Magellson has been ill during the winter-that is a shame. I hope that he is better now?Please give him my very best wishes.Also my regards to every one else in Northport,and between Northport and theLake.My love to all of you-and the Fredricksons.

Eugene Masselink

Note: Eugene Masselink became Frank Loyd Wright's Secretary.

Chapter IV.

THE GARTHE BLUFFS FARM

Compiled by - Norma C. Fretheim

The Garte's of Surnadalen,Norge

This Garte farm is located at the fjord one half fjerd-
ing (3/4 American mile) from Surnadalen. The terrain is not too
rough that cattle can't freely pasture,although there is some
outcropping of rock with difficulties in some places in tilling
the soil. Grain crops were sometimes unpredictable. In older
times there were two farms on Garte, Övre (upper) and Nedre
(lower) Garte. It was not until the later part of the 17th
century that the two farms were joined together as one, and so
remained until 1840 when Ronnigan was separately deeded away
from the Garte farm.

Early value of the land was arrived at by keeping records
of natural production such as hay, oats, number of sheep, goats,
cattle,and horses the farm would support. Early records of the
farm production show that planting 9 barrels of oats produced
36 barrels at harvest, and 36 loads of hay. The farm supported
12 cows,9 calfs,32 sheep and goats, and 2 horses. The farm consisted of one meadow, a small gristmill, a water-powered sawmill,
some timber for firewood and saw-logs. It is strange that the
farm is said to have had no fishing rights, in the records, as
it lies right on the fjord.

It is said that in the early times the Garte's were instrumental in helping to start the Bank of Norway after the 14th
Century Black Death Plague, at which time they furnished their
silver coins.

Kristen Isaakson Garte (Garthe),born March 13,1806, bought
the farm Ronnigan from his brother Isaak, for 200 spisidaler in
1841, which had been separated from the rest of the Garte land
in 1840. Included in the deed was Kristen's right to 1/2 of the
sawmill and gristmill, and 1/3 use of other existing buildings
that stood on this farm. It seems that another brother Lars
Isaakson, had put up these buildings and cleared much of the land
before Kristen took it over. Other than that, Ronnigan was the
old summer barn and milkshed on Nedre Garte, and the name "Ronnigan"
itself is an indication that the area had been cleared and tilled
from oldest times.

Grandfather Kristen Isaakson Garthe was a sailor,owning his
own small sailing vessel,the "Synia", which he sailed and traded
up and down the coast of Norway and northern Europe. It was on
one of these trips that he picked up Grandmother Gjertude's
Dowery chest, which he redecorated for her when they were married
in 1842. He also brought home two very old Danish Bibles, one
dated 1690 and the other in the early 1700's. Kristen was a shrewd
business man and recognized as being a good mathematician.

Grandmother Gjertrude,Steinarsdotter Ansnes, was born in
1819. Her mother was Ildri Hallvorsdotter Brusethaug. She was
one of 12 children, which included six boys and six girls. Six
were blue-eyed and six were brown eyed. The parents adopted six
more children as well.

The marriage of Gjertrude and Kristen Garthe produced the
following children; Isaac, born in 1842,emigrated to America in
1867 and married Synnove Larsdotter Oien,Sept.28,1872.

Ane, born April 4, 1844, emigrated to America in 1867 with her brother Isaak. She married John Jacobsen Sept.28,1872.

Ildri, born Nov. 26, 1846, emigrated with the rest of the family to America in 1868, married Hans Peterson.

Ingri, born Oct. 13, 1848, married Christian Blacken Aug, 28, 1868.

Steinar, born March 7, 1851 , married Elizabeth Bahle Oct. 21, 1875.

Maret, born Aug. 17, 1853, married Jacob Waagbo, Oct 26, 1875.

Kristen Garthe's wife Gjertrude died in 1856 at the age of thirty six, leaving him with six children.In 1857 Kristen re-married Gjertrude Tronsdotter Steinberg.It has been said that Kristen's second wife "Gjertrude" had such a bad temper that when the rest of the children wished to emigrate to America in 1868, they would have preferred that their stepmother remain in Norway. As things turned out she also came along as well as their father Kristen, although the couple remained living separately. Gjertrude took care of Steiner'household and Kristen lived with daughters Ane Jacobsen and Ildri Peterson, until his death April 3, 1872.

Kristopher Jacobson Norbeck bought the Garte farm from Kristen Garthe when the family all emigrated to America in 1868.

Note: Several silver coins which had been made into buttons and worn by Kristen on his wedding jacket have been passed down to the great grandaughters as keepsakes.

Bumerka

From Todalen Book- pages 26-27
Greatgrandmother Gjertrude's
Residence mark

Ansnes   Brusethaug

Isaac Christenson Garthe

Isaac Christenson Garthe was born in Surrendalen,Norway,
August 28,1842.His parents were Kristen Isaakson Garthe of
Surnalsfjorden and Gjertrud Steinarsdoter Ansnes. His mother
died at the age of 36, when Isaac was fourteen years of age.
His father remarried Gjertrud Stenberg.

Isaac and his sister Ane left for America in 1867.Others
included;Lars Bahle,Tori Melkild and Stayle Johnson.Their
crossing took 53 days and they encountered many terrible storms
during their passage. There were 400 passengers aboard,of which
eleven died and were buried at sea.

They were four months in traveling before they reached
Northport,arriving in July of 1867.They had planned on going
to Chicago but the Steam ship carrying them had put into Northport to take aboard a supply of cordwood for fuel.Their first
impression in seeing Northport and Leelanau Peninsula was as a
reminder of the beautiful fjords they had left in Norway, and
here they decided to remain.

Most all the men found ready work in felling timber for
fuel needed by the steamers plying the Great Lakes. Much of the
wood cut at this time was done only by the axe,as cross cut saws
were still uncommon. Isaac had seen cross cut saws used in Norway,
so when his father Kristen and the rest of the family came the
following year to America,he had them bring several cross cut
saws which were said to be the very first to be used in the
Northport area,though they were without rakers. The first saws
can be credited with rakers were brought by Hans Peterson.

Isaac purchased land which adjoined the Village Cemetery.
He became a prosperous farmer,and it was said that he was the
first farmer in Michigan to raise over a thousand bushels of
potatoes in a single year.

Isaac married Synnove Larsdotter Lilleoien,on Sept.28,
1872. To this union were born the following children;Gertrude
(married Ole Martinson),Randi, Carl(married Lena Bahle and
lived in Suttons Bay),Stanley,a teacher(married Nora Hanson and
took over the farm),Christine (married Thomas Roy and they ran
a dairy farm to the west of the Stanley Garthe farm), Laura
(married John Hagen who was a first mate on the Car Ferry at
Northport and later established a shoe and repair store.)
John,a carpenter,married Anna

Isaac had built a Mackinac type fishing boat with Chris
Blacken,which they kept on the beach below the bluffs of the
Hans Peterson property (now Peterson Park),Their boat was stolen,
which was not to uncommon in those days.Much of this thievery
was attributed to the Mormon Colony on Beaver Island,but the
mormons had been evicted from their stronghold there prior to
this happening. The boat finally was reported to have been seen
on North Manitou Island. Isaac and Chris along with several volunteers,armed with stout clubs set out to recover the missing
boat. Isaac at this time stood six feet two inches in height
and weighed well over two hundred pounds,and it was said that
he was as strong as a horse. His partner,Chris Blacken was said
to be able to muscle a barrel of salt pork over his head. As
it turned out, this formidable group of men had little difficulty
with their advrsaries in the recovery of the lost boat.

The Garthe Bluffs Farm

Steiner Christen Garthe, born March 7, 1850 was seventeen years old when he sailed from Christiansund, Norway in 1868. Others included his father Kristen, sisters Ildri, Ingri, and Maret. His older brother Isaac and sister Ane, had preceeded them the year before in order to look over the land in which to settle.

The sturdy sailing ship (the Jonas) was thirteen weeks in making the crossing. All passengers were expected to provide their own food and do their own cooking aboard. All Garthe men were experienced sailors, and knew how to provide for a long sea voyage. They had taken along a good supply of potatoes, lute-fiske and flotbrod (dried fish and hard tack), which later was needed in sharing with others less fortunate in their planning.

During one occasion of the crossing, heavy seas rolled high over the ship, forcing open a hatch cover, resulting in sea water rushing into the galley below, extinguishing the fire and scattering all the pots and kettles with food for their next meal. Chrus Blacken, a cousin of the Garthe's had been assigned as fire tender on this day!

After the 'Jonas' had docked in Quebec, and had discharged all her passengers the ship was condemned as being unseaworthy. There had been 300 passengers aboard during the crossing, as well as three deaths and three births.

Steiner Garthe upon his arrival at Northport, being short of funds was forced to work for his room and board. In one instance he had contracted with a farmer to work and get his room and board for a year, plus $150.00. The later amount of which he was never able to collect!

Steiner was finally able to save enough money to purchase his first farm land, which was situated on the buffs, over 300 feet above Lake Michigan. The soil was a good clay loam. A section of this first parcel was purchased from an Indian whose name was She-she-bun-ga. Part of this piece, about two acres had been put into hay, with the rest being covered with a beautiful stand of hardwood timber. This little clearing later was referred to as, "She-bun-ga land". This little opening lay next to the bluffs and northwest of the present farm buildings.

Steiner set about cutting and stacking the hay, and lacking a shelter in which to sleep, scooped out a hole in the middle of a stack of hay which then furnished him his sleeping quarters. His only companions at this time being a horse which he tethered near by and a pet pig, who liked to follow him around, and foraged his own food by eating beech nuts and acorns. Steiner found a spring flowing beneath the bluffs where he scooped out a hole below and dipped his drinking water from.

Steiner Garthe and his neighbor Henning Wagbo had each bought two forties of land but then traded each a forty acre in order that their acreage would be more convenient. After Steiner had cleared his land he set out a great many fruit trees. A large number of which came from Russia, having been sent through the Department of Agriculture Washington, D C.. This shipment was shared with Stephen J. Hutchinson, M.D., Northport's pioneer doctor, who was experimenting as to the hardiness of fruit trees, shrubs, flowers, and various shade trees on the peninsula. The fruit trees which were sent had only numbers, no names given them, later when they started to bear fruit they were given names by their characteristic looks or taste, such as strawberry, banana, etc..There was one apple tree, so sturdy and yet such a sour flavor that it was called the 'Norwegian'!

Steiner Garthe married Elizabeth Bahle of Baevorfjord,Norway,
on October 21,1878. Elizabeth was fifteen years of age when she
came to America with her parents,Esten and Maret Bahle.She was
born in 1855 and died in 1930. The children of Steiner and Elizabeth include:Gertrude,b.1880 -d.1850;Esten,b.1882 - d.1940
(married Jennie(Gunhild) Einerson;Maret,b.1884 - d.1956;Christine,
b.1887- d.1978,(married Nels Fredrickson);Seth,b.1889 - d.1957,
(married Christine Talgo b.1898 - d.1982); Anna,b.1891 - d.1967;
Charles E.,b.1893 - d.1977,(married Jean Foley b.1896 - d.1946)
remarried Jean's sister Elizabeth P.Foley b.1898 - d.1983;Isaac
Ludwig Garthe b.1897 - d.1977 (married Dorothy Williams b.1902 -
d.1990); James H. b.1899 -   ,only remaining child of that
generation.One other child,Christopher died in infancy.

Steiner C. Garthe took an active part in the affairs of
Leelanau Township and held the office of Township Supervisor
for fifteen years, then after being elected Judge of Probate
for Leelanau County held this position until his death in 1912.

Charles E. Garthe,son of Steiner related the following
story as told by his mother to the children,while gathered about
about her at bed-time ,only this was told entirely in Norwegian.

"Katte sette oppe omnaa og spinning,so kom de en leta muse."
"The cat sat on top of the stove spinning,and a little mouse
came gliding along,"saying; "Du spiner fint min danne!" You
spin very fine threads,my lady,praised the mouse." The cat then
answered gruffly;"Ja,Jeg spiner sa og sa."Yes,I spin so and so!"
The story would go into how the mouse had worked so hard in his
garden all summer,weeding and slaving in order to get enough
wheat to make a fine pudding.When fall came he gathered the wheat
and had it ground into flour. After baking the pudding,he placed

it on the window sill to cool, and while waiting,a little bird
flew down and gobbled it all up. The cat then said;"Jeg skall
spise deg!",meaning;"I shall gobble you!" At which time mother
would suddenly reach out and grab one of us.

Charles E. Garthe said that after a number of newcomers
had arrived from the Old Country,they spent some time working
for Steiner at the Bluffs Farm. One of these men was John Hummelstad who later settled near Gills Pier.One day,Steiner, gave
him a hoe to hoe the corn, John was a little afraid to use the
hoe being more used to a grub hoe which was much stronger in
the handle. At noon time when he arrived back for lunch he asked;
"What those weeds were growing with such large leaves,amongst
the corn?" It seems he had hoed out all the pumpkins which was
customary to plant amongst the corn! Years later,Steiner
told how his cousin AndrewAnderson in Omena,after buying potatoes
from John Hummelstad, and had sent him a check for his commission,
which John promptly threw away thinking it to be just one of those
adds sent in the mail. Note: John Hummelstad was the son of
Gertrude Stenberg,the second wife of Kristen Garthe, who at the
time of the Garthe's coming to America did not wish to come.She
later came and lived with Steiner,keeping house for him before
his marriage to Elizabeth Bahle.Her husband,Kristen,lived apart
staying with at times with his daughters Ildri (Mrs.Hans Peterson)
and Ane (Mrs.John Jacobson), until his death on April 3,1872.

Lars and Hans Sogge also came from Norway and spent some
time working at the Garthe bluffs farm. Lars later becoming a
prominent merchant in Suttons Bay.

Steiner C. Garthe

Judge of Probate

Residence, Northport
Office, Leland
Leelanau County

LELAND, MICHIGAN.

THE GARTHE BLUFFS FARM

Steiner Christian Garthe, the first owner of the Garthe Bluffs farm, along with his father Kristen Isakson Garthe and three of his sisters (Ildri, Ingri, Maret) came to America and joined their brother Isaac and older sister Anne, who had come to America a few years earlier. The mother, Gjertrud Steinarsdotter Ansnes had passed away in 1856. Steiner was at the age of 17 when he left his homeland in Surendalen, Norway.

This was adventure - They left Christiansund the first part of April 1868 and did not arrive in Northport until August 20. The trip was on an old sailing vessel, "The Jonas" (Johan). The trip from Christiansund to Northport took 13 weeks, four months of travel, of which 53 days were spent on the ocean.

There are several accounts of this trip and some of the numbers are different, depending on who is telling the story; I will give several figures in this account and you can choose the one you like. There were between 300-400 passengers aboard, all Norwegian, during the crossing; eleven or twelve passengers died and there were five or eleven births. They each paid $15.00 for their fare. Each family brought its own provisions, bed clothes and all the food necessary for themselves for the entire journey. They slept in one large room on first deck. That extended the entire length of the ship. The bunks were double, and three tiers of them. Six cook stoves were bolted on the deck on which the passengers could cook their meals. Two quarts of water were allowed a passenger each day; all was well enough as long as the sea didn't wash over the deck and put out the fires, which happened many a time.

The ship had a stormy crossing. One storm alone lasted through three weeks and culminated in a gale of three hours duration. The ship tossed and fell, the waves lashing at it like one possessed by all the devils wanting to destroy it. Mr. Lars E. Bahle, a passenger, also told once: "I can't try to describe it. I made up my mind that our graves were there." The Captain was almost forced to relieve the ship of its masts, as the entire rail on one side remained under water. During the hurricane the passengers were forced to hang on to their bunks, and throughout the storm could not use their deck stoves except on rare intervals when the furies abated temporarily, allowing them to get a little fresh air. Truly, if one is blessed with a little imagination one can see how the young emigrants emerged from the sailboat at Quebec and viewed the "Promised Land." There all disembarked and many saw no more of each other, having various destinations in mind.

The Jonas, which was on its way to Quebec for a cargo of square timbers for Liverpool, upon docking was condemned as unseaworthy, thus making this its last trip.

To avoid Niagara Falls, our group took a wood burning train

61.

to Sarnia. Their first train journey was not a happy trip for they had to board a dirty box car with wooden benches that smelled strongly of cattle. Two nights and the better part of three days were required to make this short miserable trip. At Sarnia they waited a week for the wood burning steamer that took them to Northport harbor; at the dock they were met by Isaac and Anne, their brother and sister.

At first Steiner worked on a farm for a year for $150.00 with board and washing, the two later items he got, but not a dollar of the first. After that he went and cut cordwood near Cathead Point and on South Fox Island winters, cutting fuel wood for the Great Lake ships that docked here in those days. In the summers he worked on farms. In the summer of 1872 he worked on the Walton Branch of the G.R. and I railroad and while doing so his brother bargained for a piece of land for him. It was 40 acres to which he afterwards moved and improved and added to until it got to its present dimension and development, purchasing some from the Indian She-she-bon-ga. He first built a log house in an Indian clearing, just a little north and west of the present house. This log house was built of logs taken from the virgin timber of the Garthe farm. After the Log House was built he started the harvesting of the timber which was principally made into cord wood and marketed at Northport. After the timber was cleared off, Mr. Garthe commenced fruit culture and was probably the first man in this part of the country to try raising cherries and the first to plant sweet cherries which started an opening of the vast orchards which have made Leelanau and the adjacent country famous, an added feature of Mr. Garthe's foresight. This has continued to be the business of the Garthe Bluffs farm, fine fruit trees that annually produced a great variety of fruits. Steiner was an extreme lover of all kinds of plants, some are still evident today. He experimented in fruit culture, mostly apples, grafting one variety to another in some cases. Steiner used to come to town with samples of apples and other fruits to show the feasibility of fruit culture in this section, for many old timer said that when the country was stripped of its timber that everybody would have to move to warmer climates, as general farming here could never become prosperous. Mr. Garthe was not of that turn of mind. He was endowed with good sound senses and continued carrying on developments on the farm. The products of his place were celebrated for their size, quality and flavor, and the shipments from the Garthe farm found ready sale upon the market. He was a good friend of Dr. Hutcheson; both of these men were interested in planting new and varied varieties of trees and shrubs.

On October 21, 1878, he married Lisabeth Estensdotter Bahle; she also was a native of Norway, born on the 11th of December, 1855. She was a young maiden of fifteen summers when she came to America with her parents, Esten and Maret Bahle, in 1870. They came on the "Ellen Line" to Quebec. Their journey on the ocean took only 13 days. After arriving in America she took work at DeGolier's boarding house (the Little Hotel) near the creek, for a time, also at Perry Hannahs in Traverse City for some time. Then she went to Chicago and was "second girl" at the Armour home, she stayed till her sister Maret should take confirmation lessons, and was sent down to Chicago to get her instructions and live and work at the Armour home.

As time went on the old house gave way to a more modern frame building; it was built around 1883. Mr. and Mrs. Garthe became the parents of 10 children: Christopher, who died in infancy, Gertrude, Esten, Maret, Christine, Seth, Anna, Charles Edward, Issac Ludwig, and James Hendrik.

As the boys were getting older and able to shoulder the hard work, the father began to exert his efforts in other directions. The Garthe home became a center of social, political, religious and agricultural activity for the whole neighborhood. Mr. Garthe took an active part in the affairs of this county, holding the office of Supervisor of his township for fourteen years. He also served as Probate Judge of the County, a position he held at the time of his death. He was a most diligent officer (Probate Judge) and never signed his name to anything that was not absolutely just and right. One of his characteristics was to move quickly and he would often walk from his farm to the county Seat 12 miles away, rather than take the time to hitch up and ride, for he wanted to be on the job in time. When his daughter Gertrude became old enough to handle Jenny the driving horse, he would let her take him as far as Novotny Road, (about halfway) before turning around; she would wind the lines around her hands, for she knew when she turned around Jenny would take off at a gallop and not stop till she reached home; Gertrude would hang on so hard that she would have deep creases in her hands upon arrival at home.

His sons and daughters remember the two or three day sessions of the Board of Review which brought George Craker and Henry Scott to their home to go over tax rolls and hear complaints. Mr. Garthe was prominent and influential in public affairs and his opinions carried weight among his neighbors because he was known to be a man of patriotic spirit, of progressive views and of high ideals. His children also remember when the farm home was used as a parochial school for the Bethany Lutheran Church children under the direction of the Rev. John J. Maakestad. "There were children all over the place, upstairs and down." Both he and his wife were devoted members of the Lutheran Church and in its work he took a very active part. Before the days of organs he led the singing in the worship services. At a church meeting one day at the Garthe home, it was decided that something new should be served for a lunch. It was decided that ice cream would be a treat; one older Norwegian gentleman sat by the south windows in the dining room in the full sunlight and stirred, and stirred, and stirred his till it all melted and then and only then did he eat his.

One of the old Norwegian customs that was followed by Steiner
Garthe was at Christmas time, the children were sent to bed
on Christmas Eve, on Christmas Day they knew that in the morning
the sliding doors to the living room would be closed and only
when all the children and family were ready would the doors
be opened and there would be the Christmas tree in the middle
of the living room and would be all decorated. Then they would
all join hands around the tree and they would sing, "Jeg er
så glad haver julekveld". Lutefisk was always served at
Christmas time, the dried cod being sent over from Norway.
It was soaked in a lye solution till it swelled up to its
original size, then washed and cooked.

Daughter Christine would often tell her daughters about the
nice warm and sunny day each spring or early summer when all
the bedding and winter clothes were gathered up and packed in
baskets, tubs, and whatever they had and the whole family was
called upon to help and everything was taken down the bluffs
where a fire was built on the beach and water heated and the
clothing was washed, scrubbed on the scrub boards and even some
times a stone was used to pound a bit on the severely soiled
areas. After rinsing well they were rung dry as possible and
laid on the stones and bushes to dry. At the end of the day
and the clothing was dried it was packed up and the trek up
the bluff was taken. Now you must remember that the clothing
was not wash and wear, but as Aunt Gertrude would say, "All
wool and a yard wide."

Fruit trees were not the only thing that was raised on the Garthe
farm; there were some cattle, pigs, horses, chickens and some
sheep. Sheep were raised for the wool, to card, spin and knit
all those wool pieces of clothing that were worn in the winter
to keep them warm. There were always a few black sheep, these
were to add to the white wool to make gray yarn.

The Farm had its own electric plant, a large gas powered motor
in the back shed. This suplied electric current for the Log
Cabin, farm and cottages. It was very noisy and greasy.
Electricity came in around 1940.

Lisabeth's father, Esten Bahle, made her a loom and the family
made many rugs for the home there and later to sell in the Log
Cabin. The farm made this family very self sufficient, much
of its food and income coming from it.

Almost sheer from the water's edge, where Lake Michigan laps
at the shore of Leelanau County west of the village of Northport,
clay cliffs rise 200 to 300 feet to form the Bluffs, thus giving
Garthe Bluffs farm its name. Picknickers scrambled down the
precipitous trail to build their campfires on the level sands.
Eagles soared overhead, the Great Lake whispered in the summer
breeze, or roared an angry reply to the storms that sweep its
surface. It wasn't long before the army of vacationers who
visited Leelanau County each summer became quite familiar with

the panoramic views and scenes of this wonderful lookout. It
is this grim creation of nature that gives unique distinction
to the Garthe farm, lying placidly atop the plateau, a most
wonderful scene on a clear evening when the sun is setting down
over the crest of the opposite shores. Near on the edge of
the bluffs a Log Cabin was built by the younger Garthes to make
this a most unusual farm. "The Log Cabin", built in 1919-1920
in the shape of a cross, and later added to, served many a meal
and attracted many guests over the years. It was run by the
farm family and later by their descendants, till in 1953 it
was run for the last summer. What fond memories we have of
our days swimming in the waters blue off the bluffs, and basking
in the sunlight on the shore, digging out the spring at the
base of the washout and seeing the cool bubbling water coming
up and getting a refreshing drink of that clear water. There
have been haunting calls from the Great lake in the night, and
the rotting ribs of the tug George Rogers, out of Cheboygan,
remind of days when shipwrecks were common.

The Garthe Boys set nets and were good fishermen, catching large
lake trout and white fish. They carried the fish up the bluff,
what a job; a rope was put in around the gills and they were
tossed over the shoulder and carried up, some of the fish were
so big that their tails would drag on the ground. Later they
rigged up a pulley and hauled them up in boxes with the tractor.
These fish were salted down in the fall by the family and
neighbors in salt brine in large crocks and used in the winter
for fish balls and chowder. The extra was packed in ice and
in large fish boxes and shipped to the markets in Chicago.

When Charles was older he purchased the John and Aunt Ane Garthe
Jacobson property, just west of Northport, that we called the
Swamp. The present owners are James Levy and Lois Counterman.
He lived elsewhere but spent many week-ends there with his wife
and family. Since the Garthe farm didn't have much pasture
land, the cattle from the farm were driven down to the Swamp
for the summers. A call on the phone would come in the morning
of a nice day in spring and we were alerted that the day had
come when the cows would be driven down. Be on the look out
for the cattle, so out by the road we would go and help get
them by the house and fields near our home. The boys, as they
were called, (Jim and Seth) would go down morning and night
to milk the cattle then for the rest of the summer till they
were driven back in the fall.

I remember when Aunt Maret was very sick in the downstairs
bedroom. The room that was Grandpa Steiner's office in the
early days. Dr. Bolan came to see her. Upon leaving he thought
the door out was in the Northwest corner. There was a door
there, he opened it and was ready to step out when he realized
it was the basement stairs. Quickly he took a flying leap and
thank goodness the door to the back shed was open and he landed
in the back shed.

The Garthes also had a house in town, "The Town House" as we called it. They lived there in the winter, and the boys would ski, walk, or go out to the farm to feed the cattle each day. They really ended up with two houses, the one I'm sure has some log walls under it, it is still standing today; it was sold to the Bruce Nelson family years ago and has had a number of owners since. The house that the Garthe family kept may have been a part of a barn at one time, these houses located on Nagonaba Street, across from Trinity Church. It was in later years moved up to the northwest corner of the Bethany Lutheran church lot. There it was remodeled and after Gertrude and Maret had passed away, Anna sold it. During the years that the sisters lived in the newly remodeled house they took in room and boarders, mostly school teachers, and occasionally someone from Northport Point, who came while they were building a new home on the Point. The latchstring was always out at both the town house and the farm to both old and young and their gracious hospitality will remain a cherished memory to all who had the good fourtune to share it.

After the death of Steiner his sons Seth and James took over the running of the farm; after Seth's death James continued on the farm. And then a grandson of Esten's became the fruit grower and today has purchased the farm and continues in the fruit growing.

Steiner was classed among the representative citizens and leading men of this portion of Michigan. He was born the 7th of March 1851 and died the 23rd of June, 1912. He had been having stomach trouble, it bothered him often and was perhaps the cause of his death. Mother always mentioned that he hiccuped for a long time before his death. He was 61 years of age. Steiner Christian Garthe, the young emigrant from Norway, did many things and his decendants are many, at the time of his death his obituary read, "His death was a heavy loss to the community where he lived as well as to his co-workers at the County Seat. Thus the man whose life was in the interest of mankind still lives in the memories of all who knew him."

Lisabeth, born 11 December 1855, in latter years was diagnosed with diabetes, and I'm sure this condition contributed to her death on the 7th of April 1930. She was 75 years of age.

Now a bit about each of the 9 living to adulthood children.

Gertrude: born 4 August 1880, and died 16 August 1950. did not complete her schooling, she was needed at home to help with caring for the rest of the children. When she was 18 years old (around 1898-1910) she opened her own Millinery shop in Northport, in the building that now is The Little Finger. When the Log Cabin opened she was the chief cook, and a wonderful one she was. The Garthe girls also took in room and boarders in their town house. She was very active in church activities and used her knowledge of cooking and serving meals at many

a church dinner. The Garthe girls were a quartet, and sang
at many functions in Northport and at many a funeral; Getrude
sang bass. She died of Carcinoma of the Liver, at 70 years
of age.

Esten: born 8 August 1882 and died 27 March 1940, bought a farm
not far from the Garthe home place. He married Gunhild Einerson
and they had 8 children, one passing away when just a babe.
He helped many neighbors with their fall butchering, he was
a kindly man and loved nature and his family. He died of
Coronary Thrombosis Myocarditis. He died too young at the age
of 58.

Maret: born 9 November 1884 and died 5 March 1956. She graduated
from Northport High School in 1904, she was a teacher, teaching
at Oviatt, Lautner district, the Bight, Northport and Suttons
Bay schools. She worked in Washington, DC during WWI for the
War Department - Office of the Chief of Ordnance - from April
6, 1918 to April 4, 1919. She helped out at the Log Cabin
summers. She was interested in world affairs, loved reading
Time magazine, and keeping up on literary writings. One of
her prize purchases at the farm house was the front door and
side windows; they had beveled glass, which they thought made
them extra special. She sang alto in the girls' quartet. She
had many bouts with ulcers, and Brights disease; she died of
Nephrosclerosis, at the age of 72.

Christine: born 2 March 1887 and died 1 August 1978. Married
a neighbor, Nels Fredrickson, had 4 children, one daughter still
born. She only went to the 3rd grade in school, was needed
at home. She worked at Ingalls Bay, a number of families came
from Marshalltown, Iowa and banded together and had a dining
room where they all ate their meals, they hired some young girls
to cook and serve the meals; she often talked about Clemewell
Lay, and we still have the Congregational Church Cook book,
Marshalltown, Iowa, with its stained pages, dated December,
1914. She also worked at Sunset Lodge in the Laundry before
her marriage. She sang soprano in the girls' quartet. She
died of Colon Cancer at the age of 91.

Seth: born 29 January 1889 died 17 March 1957. Married a
neighbor girl, Christine Talgo, one child that died near birth.
Seth served in the Coast Guard at Manistee. Ran the Bluffs
farm and became a fruit farmer, director of Cherry Growers Inc.,
and Farmers Mutual Fire Insurance Co. Dogs were important,
Peggy and Kai; once when Seth and Christine went to Florida,
Peggy lay by the road waiting for Seth; she didn't even want
to eat - where was Seth? - She was a one man dog. Seth in later
years remembered numerous occasions when it was necessary to
ski to Northport. Once it was to take butter to the village
when deep snow blocked the roads and the railroad for weeks
and the townspeople ran out of butter. Another time was when
cream accumulated and the only way to get it to market was over
the tops of the drifts, a five gallon can strapped to his back.

The Garthe woodpile has supplied fuel for many a freezing family of the Indian settlement in the dead of winter. He had Parkinson's and had gone to Grace Hospital in Detroit for surgery, He never came out of the anesthetic and passed away. Died of Intracerebral Hemorrhage. Age 68 years.

Anna: born 25 August 1891 and died 22 April 1967. Graduated from Northport High School in 1911. Went on to Ypsilanti State Normal College. Got her music teacher's certificate in June 1915 and a Bachelor of Science degree in March 1932. She was organist in Bethany Church and taught piano, was an art teacher and also taught grade school in many county schools and also in the Flint school system. Helped out at the Log Cabin. She sang 2nd soprano in the girls' quartet. She died of Subendocardial hemorrhage - (Coronary), Arteriosclerotic hypertension (Cardiovascular) Arteriosclerosis, Rheumatoid Arthritis and Congestive heart failure. Age 76 years.

Charles Edward: born 11 September 1893 died 22 April 1977. Married Jean Foley; they had four children; Jean passed away in 1946, later he married Elizabeth Foley, sister of Jean. In 1927 he and his brother, I. Ludwig founded the Grand Traverse Metal Casket Co. He was a veteran of World War I, a graduate of Michigan State Agricultural College. Active in his church and helped out at times on the Garthe Bluffs farm. He died of Leukemia at age 84.

Issac Ludwig: born 23 July 1897, died 15 March 1961. Married Dorothy Williams and they had two children. Along with his brother Charles founded the Grand Traverse Metal Casket Co. He was very active in the local city and civic affairs of Traverse City. Was an avid sportsman and loved hunting and fishing. He died of Pancreatic Cancer at age 64.

James Hendrik: born 26 April 1899 and died 19 May 1998. He spent his entire life (with the exception of a brief period when he worked on a carferry out of Ludington and his last years at the Masonic Home in Alma, MI) on the Garthe Bluffs farm. He enjoyed peddling fruit. He died at the age of 99, after breaking his hip and having hip surgery.

For more information refer to "The Log Cabin Meals By Appointment" Compiled by Norma Fretheim and "Steiner Christianson Garthe" Family Tree Book Compiled by Carol Drzewiecki.

Charles Garthe had received a Norwegian song book, inscribed with his name, printed in Oslo, dated Nov.21,1909. This had been given him after completing his confirmation and joining the Synod Lutheran Church, and had been confirmed in Norwegian. Steiner, his dad was the 'klokker' (song leader or kantor), leading the congregation in the singing. This was done in the early days without an organ or instrument of accompanyment to help with finding the right pitch. Uncle Hans Peterson was the 'klokker' in the other Lutheran Church -the Conference Church. One Saturday Uncle Hans visited the Methodist Church for a service of worship. The Methodist Church was in its final stage of completion under the watchful eye of Deacon Dame. At this service it was noted that Hans made the rafters ring with his loud, "Amens!" He was known to have a strong bass voice, but it was possibly aided by a nip of brandy, prior!

The Log Cabin "The Bluffs" Restaurant

The Garthe bluffs became such a popular place for picnicing and many who came to see the sunsets over Lake Michigan, along with the view of the Manitou and Fox islands and ship traffic on the lake. The Garthe family decided to build a log cabin and run a restaurant business. The log cabin was started and completed in 1920, shortly after Charles was discharged from the Army. Charles had enlisted in the Army after having graduated from Michigan State Agricultural College in 1917. He had trained at Camp Custer with a cavalry unit but was unable to travel to France in World War I due to a bad case of the flu. Charles designed the plans for the cabin with the main section measuring 26'x20', with two wing sections forming a cross at the middle measuring 12'x12'. Another larger section was added for the kitchen in 1921. Erling Bruseth also assisted in the construction.

Seth and Christine Garthe
with Elizabeth

Seth and James Garth
Picture by M.P. Stewart   Nov 14 1942

Seth and Christine Garthe,along with brother Jim,began to sell off shore property on Lake Michigan during the early 30's. Harry A. Scheiss,D.D.S., and his wife from Gary,Indiana,bought what was referred to as "The Heights".It is now owned by Charles and Barbara Yearn. A southwest corner of this property has been recently sold and new construction of a cottage started.

A section acquired from the family by brother Ludwig and Dorothy Garthe,who built a log cabin and spent summer months there for a number of years was sold by them to Ray and June Peterson. Their daughter married an author by the name of Larry Woiwoode. His book entitled: "What I'm going to do,I think" was not too complimentary of the farm scenes he depicted about the Garthe farm.

South of Ludwig's Sweet cherry orchard,was property sold Grace Cochran,Ruth Updegraff and Janet Cummings.These were all college teachers from Iowa City,Iowa. They were often referrred to as the "Iowa Girls". They called their cottage; "Cherry Bluffs".

A cabin was built south of the Log Cabin Restaurant,by the Garthe's,which was called 'Jim's Cabin'.It was a favorite place to hold Garthe family reunions,as well as being rented during the summer months to relation or other friends.It was sold to Miss Aurilla Wood and Irene Jennings of Gary,Indiana. In recent years it was purchased by Jean and Don Attwood.Since Mr.Attwood's death it is now owned by their son.

North of the Log Cabin Restaurant is the cabin built by Grace Stafford,Margaret Southwick, and Louise Eberlein,a sister to Margaret Southwick. All came from Gary,Indiana. This cottage is now owned by Jane Schwertfeger.

Charles E. Garthe had acquired the Garthe swamp farm, which adjoined the western most part of Northport, and which in earlier days provided good grazing land for the Garthe herd of milk cows,during the summer months.After which they were brought back to the Bluffs farm.

In 1925,brothers Charles and Ludwig Garthe along with Aleric Raymond,started the Grand Traverse Metal Casket Company in Traverse City.Aleric Raymond had previous with a casket manufacturing in Chicago.His wife Annie,the daughter of Ildri and Hans Peterson, was their second cousin.At this time,Charles was employed by the New York Railroad as fruit inspector.The Charles Garthe family thereafter spent their week-ends at the swamp farm.

Events since the death of Christine (Mrs.Seth Garthe) in 1982, and with her brother in-law James taking up residence at the Masonic Home in Alma,have resulted in the sale of the rest of the Garthe Bluffs Farm..The first of these parcels to go being the property with the Log Cabin Restaurant, sold to Barbara Gentry,in 1990. So ends the story of the once proud farm established by Steiner C. Garthe.

The 'Log Cabin,The Bluffs Restaurant' became an entire
family operation including;the preparation of the meals,dress
ing the chickens,setting of nets for lake trout,raising the
vegetable garden,baking of rolls,bread,cake and pies, as well
as the making of the home made ice cream in the large gasolir
operated freezer. These dinners became so popular to the summ
resorters, that it became necessary to call ahead for reser-
vations. Many of the neices and other relatives helped as
waitresses. The business flourished until August 31,1953,wher
it became necessary to close due to the ill health of the aur
ies, at which time they had served 14,500 meals.

Aunt Maret who had worked in Washington D.C.,during
W.W.I., and also taught school at the Bass Lake Country Schoo
near Omema, was the hostess.She would show visitors the dower
chest of their grandmothers which had been brought from Norwa
and given to Kristen Garthe's first wife Gjertrude Ansnes,
upon their marriage. Maret also decorated the tables and the
cabin with fresh floral arrangements ,cut from the flower
garden, and made the individual salads for the meals.

Gertrude the eldest,had a hat shop in Northport for
many years,was the main cook for the meal of soup, vegetables
chicken,fish,or steak, rolls,and desserts.

Anna kept the Aunties home in town,did the grocery
shopping and taught school away during the school year.

The cabin was open only during the summer months as
was not winterized. Two fireplaces served to heat the cabin
on the coldest days. After its closing the cabin was occasior
used by the Bethany Lutheran Church serving smorgasborg dinne

A Garthe Family Gathering
Jun, 1933

During the 1930's, Seth and Christine Garthe had several summer boarders at their farm home. Eugene Masselink came several years from Grand Rapids. He was an accompished artist and painted many landscape scenes about the Garthe bluffs. He took an interest in teaching my sister Margaret and me in painting with water colors. Eugene Masselink later became the private secretary to the noted architect, Frank Loyd Wright.

The Garthe brothers, Seth and Jim, ran a successful fruit orchard business, but the setting of fish nets was discontinued in the late 30's. As Charles said; "It was strenuous work carrying 70 pounds of fish on ones back up that steep trail from the beach below." Charles finally contrived a system for hauling the fish up an easier way, by means of a taught cable fastened to a huge rock on the shore and a good anchorage above. With block and other tackle they brought up the fish in boxes aided by hooking cable to a car which pulled them up much easier.

The Garthe farm which once had over a mile of Lake Michigan frontage, had once been the homes and land holdings of the following Indians; Joseph Nis-saw-o-quet, Theses Missabe, Meo-sin-naw, Now-com-go-quay, John She-she-bon-gay, Waonogna Mutchiseepe, Ekin Okinsbego, and Paul Nisowoquet. None of these names can be found of descendents living in Leelanau County, today.

Northport's Beginning

" Old Mission to New Mission"

According to Dr. Hinsdale Author of "First People of Michigan";quote: "When the first white settlers came to Traverse City they found an Indian winter resort on the north eastern shore of is now Boardman Lake. The Indian women and children remained at this winter camp while the men hunted, fished or trapped farther inland. At this time there was a wigwam village at Omeena,whose leader was Shab-wah-sung. Another band of Indians had settled near where Leland is today, and was called by the name "Che-ma-go-bing,and sometimes called Michi-me-go-bing meaning;"Place where the Indian canoes run up the river because there was no harbor!"A Chippewa Chief "We-se-gen-do-ba" was said to have been the first Indian known to have lived in the Grand Traverse Region by early white settlers.He lived on the island in West Grand Traverse Bay now called Power Island,though formerly it had been called Marion and also Ford Island.

Old Mission Peninsula lies between East and West Grand Traverse Bays. It extends into the greater Grand Traverse Bay, a distance of eighteen miles. The Grand Traverse Lighthouse which stands at the very tip of Old Mission Peninsula lies exactly halfway between the North Pole and the Equator, at 45th degrees latitude.

It is thought that the first white men to come to the Grand Traverse Region were; Rev. John Fleming and the Rev. Peter Dougherty,Missionaries sent out by the Presbyterian Board of Missions in May of 1839.They rounded what is now called"Old Mission Point" into what became to be called Mission Harbor and landed their supplies which they had brought in a Mackinaw boat from Mackinac Island. At this time the head chief of the region ,"Aish-qua-gwon-a-ba", after hearing the intent of the Missionaries,informed them they would hold a council meeting to see if he could unite the bands together at the Mission. The meeting was held at the mouth of the river at Elk Rapids.

On June 20th a small vessel arrived in Elk Rapids with Henry R.Schoolcraft,Indian agent at Mackinac Island,aboard. He had an interpreter,Robert Graverat and a blacksmith,Isaac George, along with him, as well as blacksmith equipment. The Indians entitled to have a blacksmith and his equipment under the Grand Rapids Treaty of 1836. Schoolcraft decided to locate the blacksmith shop on the west side of Old Mission Peninsula at what is now "Bow ers Harbor". It was not long after the departure of Schoolcraft that the Chief approached Rev. Peter Dougherty to inform him that the Indian Band preferred to move to the peninsula. Note: It has been recorded that it was Henry Schoolcraft who is given credit for naming much of the counties of Michigan, many being Indian in origin!

In 1852,the little group of wigwams and log cabins in the Old Mission harbor had grown into a village of considerable size.The Indian had now abandoned their earlier style of wigwam home and were living in houses built of hewn logs which were white washed on the outside. The Grand Rapids Treaty of 1836 did not give the Indians any title to the land,and the peninsula itself having been reserved for their exclusive occupation for only a period of five years, after which they would be at the pleasure of the U.S.Government.The lands of the peninsula were held in sufferance and liable to be taken away at any time.A deputation was sent to government held lands in the west to be examined as their new home site by remaining Indian Bands, which resulted in proving very unpleasant to them. They determined not to be removed, and with some Indian families preferring to take refuge in Canada. At this juncture a loop hole was found in the adoption of a revised State Constitution of 1850 which made citizens of all civilized persons of Indian decent,and members no longer of a tribe. This seemingly would be a way out of the difficulties as they could now purchase land from the government as citizens. The land of the peninsula was not yet on the market,but lands on the West side of the Bay, in Leelanau,were. On the advice of Peter Dougherty,families agreed to set apart a certain amount of their annual payment monies for the purchase of land.Chief Ahgos took a list of names he was authorized to receive annual payments to the government agent at Mackinaw.With these funds land was then purchased in Leelanau County,from the U.S.Governments land office at Ionia. It was in the spring of 1852 that Rev. Peter Dougherty moved the Indian Mission to New Mission at Omena. The mission to the Chippewa Indians was then thirteen years old when it was moved across the Bay.

In 1851 by an act of the State Legislature and approved on April 7th,the part of the Territory which had been formerly referred to as "Omeena",was then declared "Grand Traverse". The whole of the region prior had been referred to as "Omeena". This Indian word is said to have been coined by the Indians, meaning;"Is that so?" This having been attributed to being used by Rev. Peter Dougherty,so often after hearing questions posed by his congregation!

The Rev. Peter Dougherty ran the New Mission until the year 1871 when it closed due to lack of Mission funds,and Rev. Dougherty was then assigned to a church in Wisconsin. A lovely architecturally constructed Presbyterian Church still stands in Omena and symbolize the many years of fruitful service that the Rev. Peter Dougherty gave to his Indian Congregation. Services of worship are held there during the summer months.

In 1854 there were about 500 Indians living in the Grand Traverse Region. In a Leelanau County Atlas of 1881 it shows many land holdings which had been purchased by Indians, but by the 1900's much of these lands had passed into the White man's hands.Much of this can be attributed to unscrupulous dealings with white merchants,and in many cases in the Indian himself in being unable to read,write,or carry out his own transactions,being unfamiliar to present farming practices.

Rev. George Nelson Smith

Rev. George N. Smith, founder of Waukazooville, which later became a part of Northport. This biography, written by the late N. C. Morgan who knew him well, perhaps most vividly portrays the real personality and courage of the man of whom so much has been said and written.

He exerted a great influence on the community during his life time and in the early days was the community's host to all notables who came to town--preachers, lawyers, judges-- all were entertained by him.

When Horace Greeley sent Mr. Meeker of his editorial staff to establish Greeley Colony in Colorado, he stopped off at Northport on his return trip and paid Mr. Smith a call. Meeker Mountain in Colorado was named in honor of this man.

At the time of the excitement caused by the execution of John Brown for his attempt to free the slaves, Brown's brother, who was a cousin of Mrs. Smith, found a safe hiding place at the friendly Smith home until quiet was restored.

REV. GEORGE NELSON SMITH

Father of Northport and one of the earliest settlers of Michigan.

How any person regardless of health, strength and ruggedness, or experience in the wilderness, could have endured the privations, obstacles and destitution incident to a backwoodsman and come through it all without disabling himself and family seems almost miraculous. Yet just such conditions were experienced by the young Smith family with whom I was acquainted for many years. Mr. Smith used to relate occasionally some of the trials he had been through, but it was among some of the writings of his granddaughter, Mrs. Etta Wilson, that I gleaned the details of his life. Mr. Smith was a native of Vermont being born at Swanton in 1807. The male members of the Smith family were intensely patriotic and had served in the Revolutionary War and also in the War of 1812.

Of the childhood of Mr. Smith, little may be said excepting it was barren of the pleasures which are the inherent right of the young man. His parents were pronounced Calvinists and young George became imbued with religious feelings at a very early age. During his early life, he worked on the farm and attended school winters. In 1827, he went to Highgate, Vermont to learn the trade of a millwright. The men he worked for were Universalists who sought to convert the young man to their point of view but without success. It was their zeal possibly that pointed out the way of life to the future missionary. He studied the Scriptures so zealously that in 1823 he was converted and joined the Congregational Church at Swanton. From this time he sought to qualify himself for the ministry and studied hard to attain that end. He visited an Uncle in Canada who was a physician and here he took up the study of Latin and Chemistry. About this time he became acquainted with Miss Arvilla Powers to whom he became engaged and later married. Miss Powers was

a cousin of Hiram Powers, the sculptor, and also was a cousin
of John Brown, the abolitionist. Although poor, Mr. Smith
continued his studies, his great ambition to become an ordained
minister being uppermost in his mind. He was always afraid
that he would never reach that point. His wife aided materially
by sewing and teaching school. Mr. Smith also taught school
for a time at Alburg, Vermont. Here they started their first
housekeeping. In 1831 Mr. Smith attended courses of theological
lectures which were given by the Rev. Worthington Smith.

About this time, there was considerable agitation going
on as the cry of "Westward Ho!" rang out through the New England
states. The Smiths fell in with the idea of living in a country
that furnished more milk and honey than the stony hills of
Vermont could produce. However, Mr. Smith, bent on more
learning, and Mrs. Smith's health being unfit for travel,
patiently waited until conditions seemed more practical to leave.
Their first child was born in 1832 and was named George Nelson
in honor of his father.

In May, 1833, a colony of Congregationalists was formed
to start for the far west--Ohio or Michigan being their
objective. The Smiths were determined to accompany them but
for some reason the colony failed to materialize. Mrs. Smith
was now in fairly good health and they concluded to start out
alone. Mrs. Smith's sister, Miss Jane Powers, was to go with
them. Miss Powers later became the wife of Hon. D. D. McMartin
of Kalamazoo. The party gathered together what little
necessities they had, packed them up and on the 8th of May 1833,
started for the far away territory of Michigan.

They crossed Lake Champlain by steamer and took passage
on a canal boat to Buffalo, taking another steamer across Lake
Erie To Detroit, upon which the women and baby occupied the
cabin while Mr. Smith took a deck passage.

Mr. Smith had hardly reckoned the expense of the trip
and on arriving at Detroit found that he had only one dollar
and six cents left and still had a long distance to go, for
Gun Plains was their objective point. Fortunately they met
an old acquaintance form Vermont who took them to the only hotel
that was kept by a Frenchman. The building was made of logs.
This then became their advent into real pioneer life of a
wildness devoid of roads and scarce marks of civilization.
To meet the expense in Detroit Mr. Smith offered his keepsake
watch for sale. Buyers were scarce and money more so. He
finally ran across a party who offered him five dollars and
a half for it which was about one tenth of its value. Mr. Smith
was loath to accept the offer but he must have money at any
sacrifice. He then found a man who had an old team and wagon
who offered to undertake the trip to Gun Plains for twenty
dollars --payment for the amount to be guaranteed by the Vermont
friend.

Their most perilous adventure was now ahead of them. They
first struck out over an Indian trail which they followed
westward. This path gradually zigzagged into other trails
running in various directions. In some places were marks through
the deep woods showing where a party of surveyors had cut their

way through. They encountered some horrible corduroys through
the deep swamps. Many times Mr. Smith had to get out and into
water up to his waist in order to pry the wheels out of a deep
hole. These discomforts were almost unendurable.

For a week the little family battled with the tortures
of a lumber wagon, eating wet and cold fare that had been exposed
to the weather and at night trying to sleep in or under the
wagon or on some old shanty floors which had been left by the
surveyors. The entire trip from Vermont occupied twenty-one
days and cost over seventy dollars which was far above their
expectations.

Finally arriving at Gull Prairie they found nearly everybody
down with bilious fever, a fever and ague of an intensity that
shook the very hardiest. Not a house or even a room could be
found for the family. Finally they found a room at the home
of a Presbyterian minister whose wife was down with the fever.
This room was offered to them in exchange for their help in
caring for the sick woman and the services of Mr. Smith in
helping to build a barn. Thus arrangements were made for their
entertainment.

The family remained here until fall when they found a small
building that had been used for an office. This house was quite
convenient and had a large fireplace and for a time the family
had some of the comforts of a home.

The first three years were most trying ones. Mr. Smith
taught school whenever he could find someone to teach and also
did what he could at carpentering. However, all building being
made of logs, this was a kind of work that he was not accustomed
to. Whatever work he did was at one dollar a day for ten and
twelve hours.

Nearly the whole of Western and Southern Michigan was a
wilderness. The town of Marshall consisted of two log houses,
Jackson was known by its one hotel building, Kalamazoo was but
a suggestion, and Grand Rapids was principally an Indian trail
and a trading post of the American Fur Company. There was also
a Mission for the Ottawa Indians which was in charge of the
Rev. L. Slater, a Baptist Missionary. Work was being carried
on at the University of Michigan buildings. Western Michigan
was almost a trackless forest.

The winter following, Mr. Smith was appointed agent to
distribute Bibles in Kalamazoo County. He also preached wherever
he could find hearers. Miss Powers, who was teaching school
several miles distant, was taken sick and was brought home on
a bed, having been stricken with bilious fever. Mrs. Smith
was also ill and gave birth to a son who soon passed away.
The problem of living was a most serious one. Mr. Smith worked
like a slave daytimes and nights were given to his studies,
all the time with his great aim in view of becoming an ordained
minister. In 1835 he received a request to preach at Plainwell
and Otsego alternately with prospects of receiving aid from
the Congregational Society which was yet in its infancy.
Arriving at Plainwell, they found their only shelter to be the
frame of a building and Mr. Smith started at once to board it

up with green lumber fresh from a mill 15 miles away. There were no doors or windows or any material for a chimney. Quilts and old carpets were used to cover the openings. Wolves were numerous and their nightly howls kept everybody awake. In order to keep them back a safe distance, a log fire was kept burning which had the desired effect. They had an old cook stove which they had to set up out of doors until a chimney could be provided. Their bedding and clothes became so saturated that they had to be hung outside to dry. Water had to be carried from a spring a quarter of a mile away.

Finally a subscription was started and circulated far and near and enough money was raised to buy an acre of land. Lumber was also donated for a house and at once they started to build. When the house was ready to be raised, word was sent out through the country and there was a large turnout to help the student of theology. The frame was put up in one day but it took a month to enclose it. The lumber was green and the family began the dangerous task of seasoning it. They also had to be satisfied with openings for doors and windows and a chimney was out of the question. A spot was left floorless where they were to have fire, the smoke escaping through a hole in the roof.

There was now another baby born, a daughter whom they named Mary Jane. Both children were stricken with pneumonia and for several weeks just lingered, but finally recovered.

The bleak weather was upon them and still no chimney. Finally Mr. Smith undertook to build one of sticks and clay mortar, and completed it. It served its purpose but had to be carefully watched.

Then followed one of the most dreary winters imaginable. Starvation was threatened. The Missionary Society's means were limited and the farmers were poor and almost helpless. The Smith's home was located near the main travelled road and here wayfarers stopped either for a bite to eat or a night's lodging, or to inquire the way to their objective point. Often after a meal was eaten they did not know where the next was coming from, yet there always seemed to be some replenished miraculously as was the descent of Manna for the Children of Israel.

One afternoon two gentlemen who were on their way to New York called and asked to stay all night. One of these men was the late F. J. Littlejohn, and the other, a minister. All the eatables in the house consisted of a few small potatoes and a little flour. Mrs. Smith, who was at her wits end, quietly went to her attic and poured out an appeal for help from the only possible source. Suddenly there was a knock at the door and a neighbor entered bringing a large piece of meat. The man said. "I was all tired out but somehow I felt that I must come."

Mrs. Smith's cooking utensils consisted of one very small iron kettle, a tea kettle, and a frying pan. There was nothing to boil potatoes in so she placed them in the hot ashes by the fire and roasted them. Then making a batch of dough, she flattened it out and placed it in the hot ashes by the fire until it was nicely done. Young George was sent to a neighbor's for milk from which gravy was made. When the meal was over, the guests declared it the best meal they had ever eaten.

MATTERS BRIGHTENING

The next year conditions began to improve and they finally had the windows and doors put in. Sunday services and mid-week prayer meetings were better attended. The Home Missionary Society sent one hundred dollars and pledged the same amount for the year following.

In 1836 the Young Student was licensed to preach at St. Joe, Bronson and Comstock. He organized Congregational societies at Gull Prairie, Otsego, Plainwell and Gun Plains. He preached alternately at all of these places, preaching three sermons each Sunday, often many miles apart. His salary amounted to two hundred dollars a year and voluntary subscriptions. He took a prominent part in nearly all conventions held in the district and became deeply interested in the total Abstinence Society at Marshall.

In 1837 his great aim was attained. At a meeting of the first Congregational Association held at Richland he became ordained by Rev. A. S. Ware, making him the first Congregational minister ordained in the State. The Rev. Samuel Ballard was the second to be ordained. Mr. Smith now was a fullfledged minister, his great desire having been accomplished.

It was during this year that the conviction grew on him that he was called on to labor in behalf of the Indians. About this time a company of Ottawa and Ojibewa Indians came down from Middle Village in Emmett County in search of a Missionary. They had come under the direction of Chiefs Shine-go-che and Waukazoo. The Indians had been under the direct tutelage of the Jesuits but were not satisfied and wanted to embrace Protestantism. A meeting was held in Allegan and Mr. Smith attended. Chief Waukazoo made an impassioned speech, portraying the desires of his people. This was interpreted by James Pricket (a half breed Indian), into English. Mr. Smith was completely overcome with the fine rhetoric of this Red Man and the evident sincerity of the entire company. He at once concluded to cast his lot among those who were making the plea for the light and life of Christianity. He remained the Indians' unfaltering friend up to the day of his death.

Another meeting was later called at Allegan for the purpose of talking over a scheme for colonizing the Indians. At this meeting they formed the "Western Society of Michigan for the Benefit of the Indians" and Mr. Smith was appointed General Agent. Then began one of Mr. Smith's most arduous tasks. He traveled throughout Western and Southern Michigan seeking aid for this work. He called on every Indian family asking their cooperation and raising what funds he could. Everybody seemed interested and helped all that was possible.

In December the family moved to a spot near Allegan and here Mr. Smith preached his first sermon to the Indians. There were so many incidents that occurred during this long and tedious work of colonization that space will not permit mentioning.

From the time that Mr. Smith had concluded to work in the Indians' behalf, he began to try to study their language. The writer, who was raised among the Indians, learned to speak their language when a child, but has never heard of any White Man who acquired it after being grown up, to the extent that Mr. Smith had learned it. He was able to take the part of a lawyer, doctor, preacher and adviser which, of course, was a wonderful asset in the work he was to undertake. It was no trouble for me to learn it, as my schooling for a number of years was directly among them, but whenever I heard Mr. Smith talking or preaching to them, I soon concluded that I could not talk the language as he could.

Mr. Smith opened a small Indian School with seven scholars which soon grew to thirty with ages running from five to fifty. A Church school building was built and covered with basswood bark which was placed on end. There was no floor. The ground inside was beaten down hard and in the center was a place for a fire, the smoke escaping through the roof. At times as the ground became warm, frogs would work themselves inside and squat around the fire in characteristic attitude. The dusky children saw nothing particularly amusing about this. Mr. Smith used to relate often some very amusing things to me of his experiences. Mrs. Smith helped with the school, using her kitchen for a school for the girls.

The winter was filled with trials severe enough to daunt the bravest hearts. Provisions were short, but they continued in hopes of replenishing them. Mr. Smith and a White neighbor, Mr. Cowles, started out in a canoe for Allegan hoping to secure enough supplies to carry them through until spring. They paddled down Black River for nine miles and out into Lake Michigan and on to the mouth of the Kalamazoo River. This trip consumed three weeks. In the meantime Mrs. Smith and family were reduced in provisions and had only a few potatoes left when Mr. Smith returned. This was close to the verge of starvation.

By spring the Colony had grown to three hundred families and there was an imperative need of a permanent organization. In April 1839 Mr. Smith, with a party of Indians, started out in their canoes on a prospecting trip, which extended from the mouth of Black River north to Cross Village in Emmet County. This trip occupied four week.

They then decided to locate along Black River, east of the present site of Holland. During the summer all of the Colony moved there. Here was established "Old Wing Mission" named in honor of an old Indian, a pronounced Catholic. The work for the uplift of the Indians was now being centralized and was carried on for ten years. Mr. Smith doctored the sick and settled their disputes. His word among his simple minded people was law. His duties were varied and exacting and his reward was accumulating in Heaven.

In 1847 a colony of Hollanders from the Netherlands came and settled at Black Lake. This was an advance guard of the great army of Dutch who followed later. They had started from the Old Country in 1846, their objective being Wisconsin. They were under the direction of the Rev. A. C. VanRaalte, the man who in later years became familiarly known throughout Western Michigan. When the party arrived in New York, they ran across a Countryman who had traveled quite extensively and he persuaded them to try Western Michigan, for by this time there were railroads and that part of the country was rapidly developing. There were also good markets.

When the party arrived at Detroit, navigation was about closing and there was no way to get to Wisconsin by water. Consequently they decided to remain in Detroit until conditions were better for traveling overland. In the meantime, Mr. VanRaalte having heard of Mr. Smith and his Mission, started out on foot on a prospecting tour toward the coast of Lake Michigan. In December, he arrived at the Smith Mission where he was entertained by the family for several weeks. By this time there was lots of snow but this did not daunt the investigation of Mr. VanRaalte, who was determined to investigate and find out what kind of soil it was and everything else that tended towards a farming industry. Mr. Smith provided him with a pair of Indian snowshoes, but the man from the Dykes was not accustomed to them nor to traveling through the snow. Yet he floundered along with determination until his efforts would nearly overcome him. He would sometimes sink down in the snow and holler, "I can no more! I can no more!" This was very amusing to the Indians who were guiding him through the woods and after they had helped him out he would start again more determined than ever. He was beginning to learn of the blazes on the trees and the mysteries of the Red Man's snowshoes. He would often dig down into the ground to find what kind of soil it was. After a most thorough inspection he returned to Detroit, accompanied by a few men among whom was Mr. Grootenhuis, who was his right hand man.

In February the entire colony returned to "Old Wing Mission" and all put up at Mr. Smith's until they had completed their houses in the spring. Here began another heavy burden to Mrs. Smith's trials. The Hollanders were used to a different way of living. However, they were educated and in their way respectable. The Indians began to feel that their rights were being molested and they complained that when returning from their hunts they found some of their belongings at their wigwams were missing. This, of course, added to their ill will which grew to be so intense that they became very discouraged and finally concluded to try and find a more desirable location where their rights would not be interfered with.

In the spring Mr. Smith and Chief Waukazoo and family started in their canoe towards the North, coasting along the shore and investigating each feasible location along the way. They went up to Mackinaw. While there they decided on trying Leelanau County and the party returned to the Mission and preparations were made for the Indians to move. The Indians then migrated in their canoes or Mackinac boats. The Smith family, the McLaughlin and Cases, altogether seventeen in number, went in the little Schooner Hiram Merrill, which Mr. McLaughlin had purchased in Chicago for the purpose. Captain Huntley manned the ship while Leonard Venice was deck hand.

This was a most memorable occasion. Mr. Smith had four head of horses, four cows and three calves, which were driven up along the shore by George Pierson, Frank Whiting and John Drewar. They were often obliged to ford streams and swamps and cutting out brush wherever necessary in that wilderness where the sound of an ax had never been heard.

The sailors kept as close to shore as possible and the only places where there were signs of civilization were at Grand Haven and Manistee. At Grand Haven the Smiths met the Ferry family who were in charge of a Mission there. These two families were old friends.

Mr. Smith had planned on his initial trip to locate at Cathead Point where he had stopped and named the location of Louisville after Louis Mc Sawba, a Mission Indian. However, they changed their minds and concluded that some place on Grand Traverse Bay would be more suitable.

On June 12, 1849, the little schooner entered Northport Harbor and in nearing the shore a short distance north of where the village now stands, they cast their anchor. The boys with the livestock took a cross country route from somewhere near Gills Pier. The landing of the Merrill was near the little point which the party gave the name of Point Lookout. The Indians of that section having heard of the White Indian Preacher who was on his way to make his home among them, had been patiently waiting for him to appear. Every day some of them were down at the shore with watchful eyes to get a first glimpse of the vessel. Finally, messengers were sent out over from the lake shore to notify those at Northport that a boat has been seen rounding Cathead Point. This report was scattered far and near, and as the Indians came down to the shore, they squatted along the bank, and by the time the Merrill arrived there was a large crowd to greet the Missionary.

The Indians who followed in their canoes from Holland were now close behind the Merrill and the entire party landed at the same time, Mr. Smith was first out and at once went among those on shore, greeting and shaking hands with the multitude of men, women and children, and saying, "Bozho," to each one. The excitement was intense. After making the rounds, Mr. Smith asked them to all draw near together while he introduced himself and those with him. Then he said "We will have our first prayer meeting right here." The Northport Indians stood in awe of him who spoke their language so fluently, for they never had seen a white person they could understand before. He told them he had come to show them proper ways of living and a knowledge of their Savior. He then asked them all to kneel while he offered a prayer of Thanksgiving for their safe arrival, and for the success of their future undertakings. Arising, Mr. Smith announced a hymn, and asked all that could to join in "Praise God From Whom All Blessings Flow". The translation is as follows:

        Mah mo yah wah,
           Mah dah mah bah—
        Wain ye zhah wain
            dah go ze yaig—
        Wa yo se mind
            wa gwe su mind
        Guh ya Pah ne
            zid o Je Cho.

        This was repeated until nearly all were familiar with it.
Mr. Smith could always strike the right key, using his old tuning
fork for that purpose. A general invitation was now given to
all who could saw or use an ax to get right to work and cut
down timber for a temporary shelter.

        The next morning the Indians appeared with their tools
and in a short time a log house was put up. Some boards had
been brought along on the Merrill, and these were used for a
floor. An old ingrain carpet was brought into use for a roof
covering. The cook stove was set up out doors. Three weeks
were spent at this camping place while a permanent house was
being built farther south. The body of this house was built
with poplar logs. Finishing lumber, shingles and doors and
windows were brought from Traverse City in the little schooner.

        While the house was being built, Mr. Smith busied himself
clearing off a spot for a garden and small orchard. They had
brought some nursery stock along as Mr. Smith was determined
that this climate was conducive to fruit culture, especially
for apples and smaller fruits. This small orchard was no doubt
the first one started in Leelanau County by a White man. There
had been a few seedling trees set out by some Indians north
of town where Muh-ke-da-wah-be-geno-je (Black Mouse) was living
at a point that in later years became the home of Oscar Kitchen.
This field was the only clearing outside of the Village.

        Thus was started the first settlement on Leelanau County,
now the midst of the greatest cherry orchard district in the
world. The thought probably never occurred to those first
settlers that this wild, bleak wilderness would ever be
transformed into what it is now.

        During the summer religious services were held out in the
open air. The three White families and many of the Indians
always attended. By fall an addition was built to the Smith
home which was used for their meeting during the winter.

        The next spring a small but comfortable log building was
put up south of the Smith home which was used for school and
church services.

                            ONOMINEESE

        About three miles south west of town was re-established
the Old Wing Mission which flourished for a number of years.
Incidentally Onomineese was the home of the writer and his mother
from 1866 to the fall of 1868, my mother being the school teacher
during that time. When we moved there, there was not a sign
of any home within calling distance. The nearest White family

was J. W. Ranger's which was about 1 1/2 miles away. The school
and home was located on a high bluff overlooking the lake.
In all other directions there was a vast forest. Was it
lonesome?

Mr. Smith came over every two weeks to hold religious
services in the school room. The Indians came for miles to
hear him expound the Gospel for he was the only White person
who could hold their undivided attention. One of the amusing
things to me and the other young children was when he used his
tuning fork to get the proper pitch for the hymns. But how
they would sing. This was their Church and they felt that they
could sing and pray as loud as they liked. It used to seem
as if their whole soul and being was blended into the words
of the hymns. I often recall the inspiration that they seemed
to get from their singing.

The first year of Mr. Smith's activities at Northport were
devoted towards the uplift of the Indians but with the coming
of Whites his scope of usefulness broadened. For several years
he was the only physician and surgeon obtainable in the region.
His services were given gladly and gratuitously. Before the
establishment of courts, he was invariably called on to settle
disputes and his decisions were nearly always accepted without
a murmur. Soon after the establishment of the Onominees school,
Mr. Smith was appointed official interpreter with a Government
salary of four hundred dollars a year. This office he held
until his death. As the population of the country increased
his labors and responsibilities also did. When the entire Grand
Traverse region was but one county, he served as   , made
his maiden speech in this building. McLaughlin and Mr. Case
each built a house for themselves. These three white families
were the first white settlers of Leelanau County.

In 1851 Mr. Smith purchased a tract of about 200 acres
of land near his home and sent his son, George, to the land
office at Ionia to perfect the purchase. A village was then
laid out and named Waukazooville after the Ottawa Chief, Peter
Waukazoo. After a new element had grown and become quite strong,
the name was changed to Northport. Then the Indians gradually
moved out a few miles from town. Mr. Smith became the first
treasurer of Leelanau County, at various periods he held nearly
all of the county and township offices. As a politician he
was not a success because of his unswerving honesty and absolute
incorruptibility. He was upright from principle and policy
never moved him. No hope of vain ever induced him to countenance
party intrigue. For this reason he was often cruelly misjudged.

Mr. Smith organized the Congregational church of Northport
and also at the Bight. While his children were small he and
Mrs. Smith taught them but when they were of suitable age,
provision was made for their higher education. The oldest
daughter, Mary, married early in life, Payson Wolf, the only
son of Chief Miengun and Charlotte Waukazoo, sister of Chief
Waukazoo. Mr. Wolf died at Cross Village in 1899. The other
children received college training at Olivet, Michigan, and
Oberlin and Urbana, Ohio. George, the only son graduated in
theology and medicine and was converted to the Swedenborgian

faith.

Mrs. Wolf was the mother of ten children and several grand-children. Arvilla was married to Joseph Voice, and after his death she married Albert Powers. Annie, the youngest of the family, married Eli C. Tuttle in 1869.

There are a number of incidents concerning Mr. Smith's life that I might relate but as I realize that this story is tiresome, I feel that I should draw it to a close. I also do not feel qualified to eulogize this noble man to the extent that he so justly deserves. However, I can truthfully say that Mr. Smith was in my estimation the most nearly perfect man I ever knew.

Out of a virgin forest this man of inflexible will had hewn out a beautiful home and around it were many acres of cultivated land. The practical work of farm drudgery was delightful to him and the fruits of his labor were spread around with a liberal hand.

Long before he felt he could be spared and years before his life work was completed, if ever such a task can be completed, the Angel of death came to carry him away to the pearl paved streets of the heaven he loved so well to describe and into the presence of the Creator he venerated. After a ten days illness, he passed away. His funeral was held three days later and was attended not only by his relatives and citizens of Northport, but by a large number of Indians, some coming many miles to place a kiss upon the face of their old minister in accordance with Indian custom. Tall and rugged Chieftains followed by their dark faced wives advanced in single file to the casket where reposed the remains of their faithful leader. They bent low and tried to fix forever in their memory the features of their beloved dead. As they turned away, tears were coursing down their cheeks. Not far from the home he loved so much, he rests in eternal sleep and by his side is his wife, who was reunited with him April 16, 1895. These people had passed on but they had left a loving memory in the hearts of those for whom they had labored so long under the most trying circumstances and who still strive to carry on their work.

By Norman C. Morgan

Several early schooners called at the little Indian settlement at Waukazooville in August of 1849:

Aug.23- Schooner Star of Roungtown came into the harbor with

her fore-mast head carried away by a squall on the 22nd.

In the evening the schooner Cherokee of Racine,Wisc., came into the harbor with her fore peak block carried away, during the same squall-both repairing.

Sept.   5- Mr.McLaughlin and I (Rev.Smith),two of his children and two of mine,George and Arvilla, went on board the schooner Merrill to Mr. Dougherty's at Old Mission. On returning on the 7th ,had another severe squall,injure to the sails.

Sept. 17- Cholera epidemic with several from Dougherty's Mission having died. Schooner Arrow arrived ,,off which bought a barrel of salt pork,price $15.00.

Note; That spring when Rev. Smith and his band of Ottawa's came north, and the schooner Hiram Merrill was rounding the Grand Traverse point, they observed a tall spar sticking out in the middle of Cathead Bay.It was later thought to have been the schooner,Kimble. The following winter when the bay was frozen solid,it is said that some of Rev. Smith's Indians came and cut off the spar level with the water,fulfilling their belief that none should know the resting place of the dead.

G.M.Dame a founder of the Cherry Home Corporation,once the largest cherry orchard in the world,voiced the beliefs of people in the vicinity of Cathead Bay;"That this section of the lake,never gives up its dead!"No lost vessel has been salvaged, though a barge loaded with coal furnished a great amount of fuel at one time, foundered off Gardiners Point. The Sardinis,sunk off Gardiners Point on Cathead Bay,was loaded with salt enough to anchor a dreadnaught.

How Northport Began

Joseph Dame was sent by the U.S.Government to Old Mission, Sept. 18,1841,to replace John J.Johnson,as Indian farmer.The next year,Mr.Dame sowed the first wheat ever grown in the Grand Traverse region . He raised a good crop that first year,which he held over until the next years crop as there were no mills to make into flour. When he had enough wheat on hand he shipped the wheat across Lake Michigan to Green Bay,Wisconsin,to have it milled.

Mr.Dame remained at Old Mission for three years and then moved to Wisconsin due to ill health in his family. He stayed in Wisconsin for seven years ,returning in 1851.He landed at Manitou Island.A fish tug was hired to take them to the mainland, and around the Leelanau Peninsula to the vicinity of Waukazoo-ville,the Indian village. There he found George N.Smith and his band of Ottawa's.He was much impressed by the good harbor,and sent to the land office in Ionia,an entry for the purchase of thirty acres of land lying next to that which Rev. Smith had plotted as Waukazooville.

In 1852,Mr. Dame with help from the Indians started the construction of a wharf,realizing the needs for the growth of the community. In 1855 he sold his interest in the dock to H. O.Rose, who then took in a business partner,Amos Fox, thus beginning the partnership of 'Fox and Rose'.This was the first dock to be built on Grand Traverse Bay,where steamers(propellers) could land. Cordwood needed by the steamers opened a new bus-iness for the new settlement.From Mill Street to the shore stood several acres of cordwood,piled eight feet high. Twenty to fifty thousand cord of wood being shipped annually.

Another dock was built by Campbell and Goodrich,sometimes called the Union Dock, was located near the front of Main street. In a report made by "Deacon Dame",who was deputy collector. the shipping made during 1864,318 propellors had called in 1861, 328 had called in 1862,and in 1863 the arrivals numbered 340. Deacon Dame served as deputy collector from 1856 until 1866.

Mr.Dame was very pleased with Leelanau Peninsula and decided to write about it.He sent a glowing descrition of the Grand Traverse Region by letter to the New York Tribune,which was published in March of 1852.The nearest post office for the region at this time being Old Mission,where mail arrived once a month.When Mr.Dame went to the post office there at Old Mission he found that he had received 64 inquiries from his article. The next month he received 44 more,and each subsequent mail day, more letters of inquiry. With the cosequent arrival of many immigrants,Mr.Dame realized the need of plotting a village site. So it was that Deacon Dame plotted Northport in 1852,with Nagonaba street becoming the town line between Northport and Waukazooville. This early twin-town arrangement,no doubt accounted for the jog in the street were Waukazoo street joins Nagonaba,which then continues to the next corner and becomes Mill street,headed north!

Waukazooville was annexed to Northport in 1852,and so it has remained.

After land had been cleared and new farmsteads started,

the cordwood business declined and schooners began making their appearances;both two and three masted types.They stopped to pick up cargo of potatoes,the first major crop.The growing of potatoes was perhaps the most important industry in Leelanau County after the lumber era had passed.The potato growing was not always profitable to the farmer,due to the fluctuation of prices,production and demand.In 1883,potatoe were 35¢ per bushel. declining to 5¢ per bushel in 1886,and then a rise to 10¢ in 1896.30,000 bushels of potatoes left Northport that year.

By the turn of the twentieth century there were few schooners left plying the village settlements along the Great Lakes,having been replaced by many Bay boats and larger ships. The Sunnyside built for the Hannah and Lay Company of Traverse City,was the first to run up and down the Bay in 1864.Captain Johnson was her captain.

A growing tourist industry was beginning to play an important transformation in the village.Tourist dollars were paying for the construction of four general stores.Two doctor offices and a hotel were built in 1881.By 1900 these business's partially supported five commercial docks.Deacon Dame had built the first hotel in Northport in 1860, and by 1894,there were four hotels in town!

The Charlevoix at left, Manitou on the right,
Center - Car Ferry, M& N.E. no.1
Photo; Elden Dame collection

Five saloons that did a flourishing business. The Leelanau peninsula was the rendezvous of adventurers, transient woodchoppers and even fugitives, and often there was excitement a plenty.

Of these early houses in Northport Mrs. Wood's tavern or Boarding house on Bay street was perhaps the most colorful. It contained a bar and a dance hall. Here Esquire Wood dispensed legal justice for at least fifteen years and when not thus engaged he followed his trade as cooper. Two sons and three attractive daughters added zest and gayety to the house. Thus equipped they could handle any emergency, socially, physically or legally.

The boys had control of a sailing vessel and were suspected of smuggling whiskey from Canada. An undercover man was on their trail. The boys, however, were put wise to it and he was way laid and pummeled unconsious with no one to witness the act.

Mr. McCabe owned the present Peter Anderson house where liquor was sold and shoes repaired. Mr. McKinley lived in the Ross Martin house where he kept a saloon. He also bought bark and did other trading. These old houses were built of excellent lumber and are in good condition today.

Near the creek stood the old Exchange Hotel which later was used as a home. Mrs. Soper, sister of O.L.White, lived here for a time.

Then in the '60's Deacon Dame built the Traverse Bay Hotel which was later called the Waukazoo. It stood on the Liebler corner and played an important part in the early history of our village - a large, plain but aristocratic colonial looking building of three stories. It always had the appearance of being well kept. Mrs. Chas. Braman cooked the first meal in this hotel. It was owned subsequently by W. N. Franklin and R. A. Campbell when it was destroyed by fire. With its destruction an important and historic land mark disappeared forever.

In this vicinity, too, in 1861 Mr. Dame built his own home, restored by his grandson S. J. Dame and still occupied by the Dame family.

The house now occupied by the Bruce Nelson family is also one of historic interest. The main part is the log house in which Miss Randall conducted her private school and stood on the corner of the late James L. Kehl lot. It was used as a carpenter shop in 1869 while the Congregational church was being built. Later it was moved to its present location by Mr. Nickles, a German.

The interesting front door on the house now owned by Mr. Bert Russell is from the first light house. The house was built by Philo Beers, 1868, who was the first keeper of Cat Head light. Brick for its foundation is also from the first light house.

The Mormons lived on the Beaver Islands in the 1850's, perhaps less than two hundred of them all told! They often annoyed the settlers by their plundering expeditions about the region. They grew so bold as to even carry off cattle. Perhaps on this account one of them was shot at Old Mission. Some of you have read the story of King Strang and his murder?

Mr Dame gives us an illustretation of their dealings. Three of them came over to trafficwith the settlers at Northport,bringing three barrels of fish in their boat.Mr. Dame had merchandise that they desired and had made a deal with them receiving the three barrels of fish and some money in payment.

After their departure he examined his purchase and found the barrels of fish to be salt and sand,and the money to be counterfeit.(For his chase after them see A.H.Johnson's little book,pp20-21.)

The Grand Traverse Light

Philo Beers was the first Light House keeper in 1848.He contracted to build the light house and he kept it for 10 years. His son Almon Beers,father of Harry Beers,was his assistant. This Light House was occupied for twelve years until 1856 ? The new Light House was contracted for in 1858 and Mr.Beers served until the new appointment of a keeper in Lincoln's administration.

The second keeper was Dr.Schertly who served until his death.He was a prominent man and something of a writer,who corresponded with Horace Greely.Assisting at the Light House for a time was Myron Woolsey,then his son took charge until a new appointment was made by the government.

This appointment was Capt.Peter Nelson who served until 1918.Then Mr.Hall,grandfather of the present Hall family, acted as keeper until the appointment of George Buttars who served for many years. He was followed by Johnson and McCormick. They were followed by McCormick and Oscar Dame;Walters and Hutzler';Cain and Leslie.

Northport's Oldest Grave

Probably the oldest grave in the Northport Cemetery is that of John Powers, born in 1789 and died in 1856. He lies in the family lot of Rev. George N. Smith. John Powers was a soldier who fought in the War of 1812, against the British. Powers was the father of Mrs. Arvilla Powers Smith and during the last battle of 1812, Mrs. Smith who was a child of seven years, witnessed this battle from a hillside overlooking Lake Erie. She had been taken there by her grandfather, David Powers a soldier who fought with Washington under General Stark.

Mary Brown, wife of John Powers who also made her home with the Smith family, was a first cousin of John Brown of Harper Ferry, being a sister to his father Owen Brown. During the Sacking of Ossawattomie Kansas, the two sons of John Brown, George and Theron visited the Smith family and urged the Rev. George Smith to join the abolitionis band. Later after the hanging of John Brown a brother sought refuge in the Smith home. When the homestead burned in 1911, a large cave which Rev. Smith had prepared for his refuge relative was disclosed, leading from the deep cellar.

The Railroad and Car Ferry

In the summer of 1903, Northport began its first railraod service to Traversee City, when the Leelanau, Manistique Railroad began operating, going through Bingham, Suttons Bay and Omena.

In 1903 a keel was laid in Cleveland, Ohio, for the Manistique, Marquette and Northern Car Ferry No.1. For several years this connected the railroad at Northport with Manistique. The old Deacon Dame, or (Fox and Rose) became the railroad dock. When the Ferry service was discontinued it became the use of the Haserot Canning Company after moving the plant from its former place at Cherry Home. After the Car Ferry Service was sold to the Grand Trunk R.R. and used in ferrying cars between Muskegon and Milwaukee. During a gale on October 22, 1929, the Miwaukee I, went down in Lake Michigan, with the loss of all crew of 52 men.

Ships of the Michigan Transit Company, including the Manitou, Puritan and other ships plying the Great Lakes stopped dropping off passengers and cargo, up until the 1930's when several tramp steamers belonging to a Norwegian Company made annual stops to pick up canned cherries from the Haserot Company and haul to the European markets.

Early Northport

In the days of pioneers, many years ago,
　Northport was　an Indian Town, they called it Waukazoo.
John Waukazoo was Mayor, and head of all the works,
　He carried out the business without a Village Clerk.
Still the Town seemed to prosper, without much work or worry,
　And hardly anyone seemed to be in any special hurry.

The Bay was full of whitefish, herring, and lake trout,
　Just drop your hook in anywhere, and pull them right straight ou
The woods contained all kinds of game, wild pigeons galore,
　No one need go hungry, although there was no store.
Indians lived a joyous life, were happy and content,
　One need not even worry, as none seemed mischievous bent!

Along in 1852, white settlers began to arrive,
　Most all the Indians skeedadled excepting four or five.
John Waukazoo stood by his grounds and would not budge an inch,
　He had a staunch supporter in Old Wind-e-go-wish.
Then there was Pete Pequoga, and John Pepequa, too;
　Who did not propose to run, "Kah win, Me no Skidoo"!

The Whites came gradually, along with several men of fame,
　Including Missionary George N. Smith, and quaint Deacon Dame.
Smith built a little church, its size was four by eight,
　And there he preached to Indian friends, about the Savior Great
He had learned the language, many years before,
　Had been sent to Waukazoo, God's blessins to implore.

Deacon Dame built the first dock on the Bay,
　Where once it stood, only pilings show today.
I can see him comb his whiskers, rub his nose, and knead his eyes,
　While us boys gathered round him, in wonder and surprise.
He told us that a railroad would come along some day,
　We only laughed and teased him, and then went off to play.

Waukazoo was changed to Northport in eighteen fifty-five,
　Then things began to happen, to prove her yet alive.
Big operations were also on, at the south end of the Bay,
　As Traverse City was a-building by the firm of 'Hannah-Lay'.
Grand Traverse Region was now opening up for sure,
　Though Northport was still the landing spot,
　　　　　　　　　　　　until their harbor was secure.

In the days of pioneers, so many years ago,
　Mail came in on an Indians back, regardless of the snow.
It came right in on schedule, he never missed a day,
　Although at times he struggled, the snow deep in his way.
Old Esquageshik, Oh so strong, did not mind a little storm,
　He was always ready for a blizzard, in any shape or form.

In 1903 Old Maude puffing came,to help us on our way,
    A round .trip to Traverse was possible in only just a day.
But when those wintry blasts did come,and too much snow did fall,
    We got our mail occasionally,and sometimes not at all.
We were thus remindful of the good old days way back,
    When mail arrived on schedule,within an Indian's sack.

As years rolled by, the Village grew to make its mark,
    Where Deacon Dame's dock once stood,is now a picnic park.
The scenic beauty of this land,is without its peers today,
    Behold the sites about you,theres none like on the Bay.
Where docks that once birthed fish tugs,and larger ships besides,
    Now boast about the harbor,where yachts in safety hide.

Stroll amongst the orchards,with cherries and apples galore,
    From Omena to the Lighthouse,and along the western shores.
Sunsets await you at Peterson Park, and there to view,
    The Manitou's and the Foxes that seem to beckon you.
There are other spots of beauty, awaiting you besides,
    Though theres none like'Old Leelanau',a fitting place
                                        to bide!
                            Original Author Unknown-
                        Revised by Wawinges-1987

Note:The box cars,the Methodist Church to the left and the
Congregational Church to the right. The old frame schoolhouse
in the center of picture. The dock being the Kehl and Nelson.

                            photo circa;1907
                        Eldon Dame collection

The following article was taken from the Leelanau Tribune
dated August 3,1873,a paper published in Northport by editor
A.H.Johnson.Quote: <u>A Strange Visitor</u>

Our town was thrown into great trepidation on a day last
week by the appearance on the bay of a strange looking vessel.
She was a long,low,black looking craft,with short,stumpy,rakish
masts - one upon the extreme point of the bow,carrying a jib
and mainsail; the other far out on the stern,carrying also a
jib and immense mainsail,which hung away out behind like a great
cloud over the water. As she moved in sight beyond Carrying Point,
and slowly sailed up the Bay, conjecture was rife among the
people of Northport concerning the character of our nondescript
visitor, and the possible object of her visit to our waters. A
crowd od idlers soon assembled at the dock and began to discuss
with much apparent alarm the probable nature of the odd-looking
stranger. A colored ex-Civil War soldier pronounced it to be a
rebel cruiser who was going to make a raid on all the villages
around the Bay, and he advised everyone to start digging sand-
pits as a protection against any shot and shells that might be
carelessly hurled among them. A meek looking clergyman then
suggested the propriety of holding a prayer meeting to avert any
impending calamity that might be coming. A venerable,round-shou-
ldered deacon declared it to be a smuggler of no ordinary capacity,
and wondered where the Customs Officers were now! A dapper little
attorney said it must be a revenue cutter sent by President Grant
to look after the interests of the administration,and gently
hinted for a liberal retainer he would defend any one who had
defrauded the government. Our lusty sheriff went prancing about
like a French dancing master , and stoutly declared he would
arrest the first one that came ashore, and take him forwith to
Northport's jail,as a dangerously suspicious person.But one
little devil, who was a wild, ambitious youth, threw the whole
crowd into a violent consternation by seclaring in his opinion
that the stranger was a Mormon pirate,and that he could plainly
see the spirits of Jo Smith,and Strang,standing amidship, between the masts, and pointing long boney fingers toward the
shore. !Twas wonderful what marvellous effects this effects had
upon the crowd. Stout men suddenly grew pale, and hurried home
and frightened there wives into hysterics, and the children into
fits. The Indians with their squaws,ponies,dogs, and pappooses,
took up a line of march for the woods and silence reigned throughout all Northport.; while the strange and weird looking craft
continued sailing on up the Bay, and passed out of sight behind
the New Mission Point,and all our people breathed easier.Whence
she came,or whither she went,no one can tell!

Some other minded individuals have been heard to say that
the strange looking vessel was nothing more than a monster wood
and lumber barge!

The Leader in Detroit

When the postman brings the "Leader"
    Dish towels,brooms and dust pans drop.
As her interest in the Leader,
    Brings her duties to a stop.

She reads what folks are back home are doing...
    Who went where,and why and when.
Not untilshe's thru pursing
    Do her duties start again.

Recipes from books of mothers,
    Household hints and funnies new,
Seems the reading's not like others...
    Sort of homelike,friendly too.

When the postman brings the "Leader"
    She can never feel alone,
For it's such a lovely visit,
    With friendsand folks back home.

                  Mrs. H.H.

Note: The Northport Leader,published by Mr. Ellis

Chapter VI

Peterson Park
ANNA RAYMOND DEEDS LAKESHORE PROPERTY AS MEMORIAL
TO PIONEER FATHER

Long considered one of the choicest summer spots in our region, and rich in historical remembrances, the eight and one quarter acres on Lake Michigan known as Peterson's Wash-Out has become a public park, thru the generosity of Mrs. Anna Peterson Raymond, daughter of Mr. and Mrs. Hans Peterson. This week Mrs. Raymond deeded the area to the Township of Leelanau with the following conditions:

"It is a stipulation of this deed that said property shall for all time remain in the ownership of the people of the Township of Leelanau; that said property shall be used for a public park, and for no other purpose; that said park shall be known as Peterson Park, in the memory of Hans Peterson; that said Township shall erect a suitable memorial to the memory of said Hans Peterson, such memorial to be in the form of a bronze plate, suitably inscribed, and securedly fastened to a stone or boulder of proper proportions, and erected on a prominent location within the borders of said land; that the said Township shall at all times keep said land in a clean and orderly state; and that as soon as reasonably possible, shall do such work and supply such equipment as is generally required in making an attractive park useful to all people".

Hundreds of people every summer drive out to the Wash-Out to view the wonderful Lake Michigan sunsets, or to enjoy steak frys on the beach. The terrain, together with the fine view of the Fox and Manitou Islands, is every bit as attractive as the Picture Rocks in the upper peninsula.

Mrs. Raymond's request that a useful public park be developed is no more than the people of the region would want to do, now that actual ownership is in their hands. It naturally follows that our Township should maintain the grounds in an orderly manner, that suitable fencing should be erected, adequate equipment, such as picnic tables, park stoves, bath house, etc., arranged for as rapidly as possible. The memorial to the donor's father, a pioneer of the region, will probably be similar to that erected at the Woolsey Memorial Airport in honor of Captain Clinton Woolsey.

Hans Peterson was born in Norway, coming to Northport in 1868. In that same year Ildri Garthe, later to be Mrs. Peterson, also arrived from Norway. They were married shortly afterwards and in 1871 settled in a log house on the farm of which this park area is a part. The old homestead is now the residence of their daughter, Anna Peterson Raymond. Mr. Peterson died in 1927 at the age of 81, and Mrs. Peterson passed away the following year at the same age.

The region around the park site is rich in Indian history, at one time there being a vilage located there. Today there remain traces of their burial ground.

Mrs. Raymond not only desired to commemorate the memory of her father, but the gift consumates a wish of many years standing, that Peterson's Wash-Out should belong to the people of this region and thereby add to the public attractions so necessary in this beautiful summer vacation land. May we, for all the people of Leelanau Township, extend to Mrs. Raymond our sincere appreciation.

1937

LETTERS TO THE EDITOR

To The Editor:
  Notes on Peterson Park,
  Northport, Michigan

This is about one of the many beautifully situated parks in our own state of Michigan, situated on a high bluff overlooking Lake Michigan, almost at the tip of Leelanau (Land of Delight) County.

Looking to the west one sees the North and South Manitou Islands, farther away to the north are the Fox Islands and on clear days one can discern the Beaver Islands in the far distance.

It is interesting to watch the large ore boats as they steam back and forth, to watch the ever changeable color of the water and at sunset view the marvelous colors in the sky and its reflections on the waters of the lake.

The park is about 2½ miles northwest of the village of Northport and covers an area of 8 acres. There are many well built stone fireplaces, tables placed under shade trees, it has a children's slide and a path goes down to the lake. The park is well taken care of and is kept up by Township funds.

It may be of interest to know why it was named Peterson Park. Some years ago Mrs. Anne Raymond donated this land to the community, to be used as a memory to her father, Hans Peterson, and an inscribed marker is erected in the park to this effect.

Mr. Peterson had owned this plot of land, together with the adjoining 40 acre tract, having emigrated from his homeland, Norway, in the year 1866, first going to the state of Minnesota and from there to Chicago, Ill. One day while standing by the water front of that city, he met Mr. William Voice, one of the early settlers of Northport, Mich., and was hired by him to go to work in the lumber woods of Beaver Island. After working there for a while, Mr. Peterson came to the mainland and bought the land mentioned, in the year 1871, from Mr. Rose, who had the original grant from the U.S. Government.

Mrs. Ida Edahl, another daughter of Mr. Peterson, has compiled a very interesting and more detailed story of the very early history of this particular piece of land.

But the main reason for writing this article was to bring out the use of the park at the present time, along with notes on the registration book kept there, for year 1956.

This book was kept in a special little booth, built on a strong supporting post. One day while enjoying a family picnic at the park, I took a look at this book and decided that sometime I would write something about the signatures of the people who had been at the park, the time they had been there and the various places they came from. So at the end of the season Mr. Eldon Dame, one of the members of the Township Board, let me take this book and I shall jot down something of what I found. It was a well bound book, such as used in hotels and covered a time from June 26, to Sept. 9, 1956.

During this period of time there had been visitors from 31 states of our United States and 6 foreign countries were represented. Nearly 1,000 had come from different places in our own state. Of course many come to the park who do not register and one must not forget the hundreds of our local people, who go there many times during the summer season.

There are always those who like to put remarks in a book like this, which they consider funny, so wasn't too much surprised to find the following names had been entered: Mr. and Mrs. Rock Hudson, Hedda Hopper, Roy Rogers and Dale Evans all from Hollywood. The Princess Grace of Monaco, Agha Kahn and son Aly of India and shades of the past, Abe Lincoln, Sherlock Homes, Adolph Hitler, Mrs. O'Leary and her cow, Marilyn Monroe also of Hollywood, had been there in July, again in August, as Mrs. Miller and believe it or not, Joe D. had been there the same date.

So many pages were badly scribbled by youngsters, some using a whole page for their name and address, again on some pages the comments would be unprintable but again so many nice remarks were made to make up for the vulgar remarks. This is just a little about one the many public parks in our state and how thankful we should be to have places like this to go to and enjoy and to remember to treat these places with respect.

I. S. M.
Northport, Michigan

The Leelanau Enterprise Tribune
August 15, 1957

TO SPEND $20,000 ON PETERSON PARK

A total of $20,000 will be spent on Peterson Park on Lake Michigan west of Northport in a join effort to develop and preserve the Park for future public use.

Peterson Park has suffered in recent years from both severe beach area erosion and vandalism both at least partially caused by humans.

Participating in a joint effort, partially federally funded will be the U.S. Soil Conservation Service in cooperation with the Leelanau County Soil Conservation District, Leelanau Township and the Northwestern Development Commission.

In the opinion of Keith Martell, U.S. Soil Conservationist assigned to Leelanau County, erosion is proceeding at a rate of about one foot a year and mother nature is fighting a losing battle to compete with human beings who misuse the Park area.

Erosion's major causes at the park according to Martell are "high water level" in Lake Michigan and "heavy use of the Park by people."

The joint project to restore and preserve the Park will include construction of a log stairway to correct the over-usage of the approach to the beach area, provision for picnic tables and an observation lookout and fence around the side of the lookout.

Another measure to keep people from further trampling the bank will be the construction of a split-cedar rail fence.

Toilets with holding tanks are also in the plans.

Martell said plans call for planting some 6,000 assorted shrubs and trees for erosion control and beautification, with additional landscaping and seeding.

"Our purpose," Mantell said, "is not to increase use of the Park but to preserve it and to control the way it is used somewhat."

Fifty per cent of the $20,000 will come from MRCD funds and 50 percent will be locally funded through the Soil Conservation District and the Township.

The SCS will pay (from part of the MRCD funding) all of the cost of the erosion control expenditure, Martell said.

Martell estimates the project will be completed by 1975. Cost of this year's portion of the project will be $7,000.

The Leelanau Enterprise Tribune
April 27, 1972

PETERSON PARK IMPROVEMENTS ENTER PHASE 3

"Phase II" of the jointly sponsored $20,000 improvement program for Leelanau Township's Peterson Park, a nine-acre park on the shore of Lake Michigan featuring panoramic views of both the Manitou and Fox Islands, has been completed.

A cooperative undertaking by the Township and the Leelanau Soil Conservation District with financial assistance from the Northwest Michigan Resource Conservation and Development Project improvements involve a three-phase program.

Improvements began in 1972 with construction of a stairway to the lake, a scenic overlook, rustic fencing and planting of shrubs, all for erosion control. Phase two, completed in the past year included construction of toilet facilities, erosion structures, signs, additional fencing and stairway.

Phase III to be completed by this time next year includes improvements on parking areas, picnic facilities and general landscaping. Some 50 per cent of the cost of the $20,000 program is being paid through the RC&D program and technical assistance for the project has been provided by the USDA Soil Conservation Service through the Leelanau Soil Conservation District at no cost to the township.

Emphasis on the rustic look has been stressed in all improvements at the park.

One ongoing project at the park will be stabilization of the bluff which the Soil Conservation District report is eroding at the rate on one foot per year.

The Leelanau Enterprise Tribune
November 29, 1973

REDEDICATION CEREMONIES OF PETERSON PARK

David Allen, Leelanau Township supervisor, speaks during rededication ceremonies Sunday at Peterson Park on Lake Michigan west of Northport. Part of the township's bicentennial celebration, the event also marked the success of the area and the Soil Conservation Service in making major improvements in recent years. The park was deeded to the township in 1937 by the Hans Peterson family.

The Leelanau Enterprise Tribune
July 11, 1976

At the rededication ceremony a new bronze plate was installed to replace the original one, that had been stolen. *n.c.f.*

PETERSON PARK...GARTHE BLUFFS....RICH IN LEELANAU HISTORY
By Martin Melkild

One of the most beautiful areas in northwest Michigan is the area which encompasses Garthe Bluffs and Peterson Park, eight acres of land located $2\frac{1}{2}$ miles northwest of the village of Northport.

Peterson Park, one of the most popular parks in Leelanau Township, was donated by Anne Raymond in 1937, in memory of her father, Hans Peterson.

The steamship on which Hans Peterson was traveling on his way to Chicago from the Old Country-Norway, had stopped at Northport, to take on a load of cord wood for fuel, before she proceeded on.

While the ship was docked, passengers were allowed to disembark, to stretch their legs, and see the sights.

Hans was loafing on the dock when he was greeted by a man in his own native language - Norwegian; "Hvordan star det til?" Meaning, "How are you?" Hans promptly replied, "Bare bra talk." Meaning, "Very well thank you."

Peter Gustaff, his new acquaintance in the new world and feeling quite worldly (having arrived several years before), struck up further conversation, by saying; "No one should go to that syrup hole of Chicago, where rum is the drink instead of straight whiskey, the likes of which should not be tolerated. Leave the rum for the ladies, whiskey is the only drink for men!"

Peter Gustaff then went on to tell how when he had first landed at Chicago, and been treated to a loaf of raisin bread. Upon breaking it open and seeing all those raisins, he thought it was infested with weevils, and refused to eat it.

He then went on to explain and praise the merits of the Leelanau Peninsula and urged Peterson to take leave of the ship and stay right in Northport.

Instead Hans Peterson continued with his paid fare to Chicago, and from there he continued on to Minnesota and Wisconsin where he worked for several years before finally returning to Northport to make it his home in 1865.

Hans Peterson who had been a hardy fisherman from the northern part of Norway, spent much of his early youth in fishing around the Lofoten Islands. While on these fishing trips they would be gone two or three weeks at a time from home. The only food taken with them was a supply of flotbrod (hard tack) and fiskeboller (fish balls) to sustain them.

Towards the end of the fishing voyage, the flotbrod would become so hard that if bitten would shatter like glass, and the fiskeboller so hard that if thrown would dent any object they hit.

It was said that this made for stout teeth, as Olaf Eiken will attest to, having worked for Hans in his youth. Hans, he said, had perfect teeth right up until his death, and he was seen to take a common file which he used if they became irregular.

In 1871 Hans Peterson married Ildri Garthe (daughter of Christen I. Garthe). They purchased 40 acres on the lake shore from Mr. Rose, and 20 acres from 'Gagnon' land, from Jacob Waagbo.

The property which is now Peterson park was land once owned by Chief George Sha-sha-wa-nabesi, leader of the natives of Cathead which adjoins Peterson Park. Not far from the Park can be found a small Indian burial grounds, even this has become desecrated and in White Man's intrusion.

When Rev. George N. Smith first came and landed at the Indian Village of Cathead, in search for a new settlement for his Indian Ottawa band, he named the place instead "Louieville" after Louis McSawby, one of his own faithful Mission Indians.

On July 11, 1976, a rededication ceremony was held at Peterson Park in recognition of major improvements to the park over a period of three years with the cooperation of the Soil Conservation Service and the Township.

. . . .

The Preview
August 22, 1988

Martin Melkild did an interview with Ray Thomas once - the following information was a part of this interview:

Ray Thomas who lived on the old Nels Blacken property near Peterson Park, recalled there was a shop across the road in the woods, where small kegs were made. This would be near the Fox View subdivision. Before the regular trout season had opened, fishermen off the Hans Peterson property would salt their catch in those kegs made at that shop. They would then bury those kegs in the sand, to escape the game warden's eye, and to sell when the season opened. Ray went on to state that the "Black Fin" fish (a soft fleshed fish) was excellent for smoking, but can no longer be found in the waters of the Great Lakes, they were all fished out.

For more information on Peterson Park and Louisville (Indian Village) see "A History of Leelanau Township" pages 23-24-211-212-and 242.

In 1994 the Garthe descendants gave donations and the Garthe Pavilion was built at Peterson Park. net.

PIONEER PASSED AWAY

Hans H. Peterson was born at Moe in Helgeland, Norway, on December 18, 1845. He came to the United States in the summer of 1867, stopping first in Minnesota. He spent two or three years in different places in the middle west, spending some time in Chicago and Logansport, Indiana, settling finally at Northport. Here he married Ildri Garthe in 1871 and settled on his farm on Lake Michigan shore where they lived for thirty-four years.

Eight children were born to them while they lived on the lake shore, four of whom are now living. These are Oscar of Manhatten, Florida, Mrs. J. A. Raymond of this place, Mrs. L.G. Howell of Troutdale, Oregon and Mrs. Ida Edahl.

In 1905 they moved to their present home where he died on March 30, 1927, aged eighty-one years, three months and twelve days.

The Northport Leader
Northport, Michgian
Thursday - April 7, 1927

PIONEER PASSED AWAY

Ildri Garthe Peterson passed away the 16th of February, 1928, at the ripe old age of eighty one years, two months and twenty days.

She was born in Surendalen Parish Oie, Norway, Nov. 26th, 1846. She came to Northport in 1868 together with her parents, sisters and brothers. Coming on a sail vessel, travel was not very fast, spending thirteen long weeks on the way. After spending a short time in Northport she went to Milwaukee, where she stayed two years; when she came back to Northport in Oct., 1871, she was united in marriage to Hans Peterson, who preceded her to his last resting place almost a year ago. To this union were born eight children, of whom four remain to mourn her loss. Oscar, of Bay City; Mrs. Howell of Troutdale, Oregon; Mrs. Edahl of Chicago, and Mrs. Raymond of Northport, who has cared for her mother more than three years. There are also twelve grand-children and one sister Mrs. Maret Waagbo of Northport.

Mr. and Mrs. Peterson settled among the Indians on a piece of land three miles north-west of Northport. This could hardly be called a farm as all you could see was logs and stumps. In order to get provisions they either had to walk or travel behind oxen, as horses were very scarce at that time. They surely went through all the hardships of pioneer days. Twenty-two years ago they built a new home one and one half miles north-west of town, where they spent their old age in more comfort. Mrs. Peterson was a life long member of the Lutherean Church and a Charter Member of the Northport Lutheran Church where she was a faithful worker as long as her health would permit. She always worked hard for her home and family. She was a lover

104.

of beautiful things in spite of all hardships. Her passing closes a long life of usefulness and hardship.

Funeral services were held at the home and from Bethany Lutheran Church Saturday afternoon, Rev. G. Guldberg officiating, speaking most comforting words, paying high tribute to the departed and much loved mother. Mrs. T.G. Roy and Miss Maret Garthe sang beautifully hymns she loved.

Beautiful floral tributes were brought as tokens of esteem. She was laid to rest beside her husband in the Northport cemetery.

The Northport Leader
Thursday - February 23, 1928

ILDRI GARTHE PETERSON

Ildri Garthe was born on November 26, 1846 in Surendalen, Christiansund, Norway. She came to America in the company of her father Kristen and sisters Marit and Ingri and brother Steiner in 1868. She worked at Hale's Corner south of Milwaukee, Wisconsin, for several years for a Dr. Sauttle doing housework. The Dr. had been a surgeon in the Civil war. In Oct. 1871 she married Hans Peterson. They bought 40 acres of land on the lake shore from Mr. Rose and 20 acres of "Gagnon" land from Jacob Waagbo. In 1906 they moved into a new house (now the Ida Edahl home). The land what is now "Peterson Park" was owned by them, the land being cleared by Steiner Garthe.

Ildri and Hans Peterson had the following children: Oscar (July 23, 1874-June 13, 1949) Charles (May 13, 1876-Apr. 22, 1889), Anne (Mar.18, 1878-Apr. 3, 1958), Gerta (Oct 29, 1879-May 12, 1950), George - , George William -, Ida (Aug 1, 1885 - Mar.11, 1989). George and George William are buied in the Kristen Garthe plot.

Bill Voice had come down from Beaver Island and gone to Chicago to look for lumberjacks. There he got Hans Peterson who had been in Minnesota and Wisconsin previously. Hans was born Dec. 18, 1845 and Died Mar. 30, 1927. Ildri died Feb. 16, 1928. Hans Peterson was a good singer. He also did fishing as they lived near the lake shore.

Peterson Park

Peterson Park,a Leelanau Township Park, lies 2/½ miles west of Northport. It is one of the nicest picnicing and sunset viewing spots to be found anywhere on the Leelanau Peninsula.It is rich in early history and in Indian lore,having been the site of the Indian village of Cathead,later named Louisville. The name, George Sha-sha-wa-nebasi appears on an early Atlas,as having been the original owner of the triangular eight and one half acres which make up the present Peterson Park lands.These lands were given to Leelanau Township for a park,by the late Anne (Peterson) Raymond,in 1937,in memory of her father, Hans Peterson.

The steamship on which Hans Peterson was traveling on the way to Chicago,had stopped at Northport to take on a load of cord wood for fuel,before proceeding on to Chicago. While the ship was docked,Hans Peterson, a new arrival in this country from his homeland Norway,was stretching his legs ashore,and was greated by a man speaking in his own native language;"Hvordan star det til?" Meaning;"How are you?" Hans promptly replied; "Bare bra,takk." Meaning;"Very well,thank you!"

This new acquaintenance was Peter Gustaff,who had arrived several years before and by now had become quite wordly in the affairs of his new country, and so went on with his conversation hoping to influence Hans,the newcomer. "No one should go to that syrup hole of Chicago,where rum seems to be the drink instead of straight whiskey,the likes of which should not be tolerated. Leave the rum for the ladies, whiskey is the only drink for men!" Peter Gustaff then went on to tell of how after he had landed in Chicago,and being first introduced to a loaf of raisin bread, and upon breaking it open thought it to be infested with weevils and refused to eat it! He then expounded to Hans on the merits of Leelanau Peninsula,and that he should take leave of his ship and stay in Northport. Of course, Hans Peterson,with his fare all paid to Chicago,not willing to lose out on that,decided to instead go on to Chicago. He spent several rears working as a lumberman in Wisconsin and Minnesota before returning to buy property and settle in Northport in 1865.

Hans Peterson born in Moe,Norway,Dec.18,1845,had spent his early youth fishing around the Lofoten Islands of Norway's northern coastline. It is said that while on these fishing trips they would be gone from home for two to three weeks at a time. The only food taken along with them was a supply of flotbrod (hard tack) and fiske-boller (fish balls) to sustain them. Towards the end of the fishing voyage,the flotbrod would beecome so hard that if bitten would shatter like glass, and the fiske boller so hard that if thrown would dent any object they hit!So it is said that this makes for stout teeth, as Olaf Eiken,can attest to,having worked for Hans on the farm during his youth. He stated that Hans Peterson had nearly perfect teeth right up until his death, and Olaf had seen him take an ordinary file with which he would file his teeth with if they became irregular!

In 1871 Hans Peterson married Ildri Garthe (daughter of Kristen Garthe). They purchased 40 acres on the lake shore from Mr. Rose, and 20 acres from the Gagnon' land, from Jacob Wagbo. The 8½ acres which had been formerly land owned by Sha-sha-wa-nebasi, was alsopurchased and makes up the present day 'Peterson Park' lands. Of this marriage, the following children were born; Oscar (b.July 23,1974,d. June 13,1949), Charles(b.May 18,1876,d. Apr.22,1889), Anne (b.Mar.19,1878, d.April 3,1958,married Alec Raymond), Gerta (b.oct.29,1879, d.May 12,1950), a George and a George William both died in infancy. Ida (b.aug.1,1885 d.   ,married   Edahl,died after reaching 102 years.

Oscar, the eldest son of Hans and Ildri Peterson, was tall with a dark complexion, having bushy hair and dark eye brows. He was a bachelor. He enjoyed singing, and pretty well carried the bass section of the Bethany Lutheran Church choir. He was a fine craftsman and ship builder, and employed by boat yards at Bay City, Sturgeon Bay, Florida, and in Northport. He owned a late model T Ford which he had outfitted with enclosed windows in order to travel great distances to find employment in those early days. He was a strict vegetarian, was well read on all issues of the day. I can remember him treating as boys to a dish of ice cream in Scott Ice Cream Parlor. Oscar himself preferred having a quart of ice cream which afterwards topped off with a quart of milk!

Oscar related the following incident of a shipwreck off South Fox Island told him by his father, as follows; "My father, had been hired along with a group from Northport to salvage cargoe from a shipwreck off South Fox Island. There they toiled getting off the cargo of barrels of salt pork.They filled every available buildings they could find on the island. My father sensed that something was not right with this salvage operation, and while sitting and waiting at the dock in Northport later, to be paid off heard whispered rumors as to the cause of the shipwreck happenings.It seems that the ship had been lured off her course by lights purposely placed to cause the accident! It is said to this day, of a family living in Harbor Springs, knowing of this event and of salt pork being peddled all up and down the western coast line of Michigan.!

In checking "Ships & Shipwrecks"Door County, Wisconsin by Arthur C.and Lucy Frederickson, I could find only one article of a ship beaching on South Fox Island.The article quotes from the Petoskey paper, the Northern Independent, of June 25, 1887: "The propeller, Joseph L.Hurd went ashore on Fox Island a few days hance and in order to get off was compelled to throw overboard a hundred and fifty gallons of machine oil, and a large quantity of beer. The lighthouse keeper is trying to recollect when he had tossed the bread upon the waters and then returned in the shape of beer!"

Chapter VIII.

The Onominees Indian Cemetery

In writing these sketches, it is not our purpose to go into historical detail so much as to relate interesting episodes and incidents that have happened in the pioneering and settlement of our township and to preserve them, to record the names of early inhabitants who have lived here and helped in the slow but steady development of our community.

Several early histories of the county have been written, "The Grand Traverse Region", historical and descriptive (H. R. Page & Co., Chicago) published in 1884, and Sprague's "Grand Traverse and Leelanau Counties" (1903) will give much information. There is also a little paper-bound sketch--not so well known--by A. H. Johnson (1880) and published for the purpose of "disabusing the public mind of the erroneous idea that Leelanau County is a barren and cold country".

More recently, we have Miss Ruth Craker's "First Protestant Mission in the Grand Traverse Region" (1931) which is especially interesting and well written.

Would that our hills and lakes had tongues to speak themselves to tell us of the thrilling adventures of this region before our pioneer fathers and mothers arrived! Then we should know who first paddled into Northport Bay and who tramped the virgin timber lands of our fair peninsula and when.

We only know that French missionaries covered, more or less thoroughly, this lake region and at one time established a village called, perhaps, Louisville, somewhere near the "Shore Acres" home of Mrs. A. J. Raymond and the Archie Scott farm, that later an Indian village called Louie Village nestled near the woods on the north side of the road, now a part of the Archie Scott farm. Today only a small burying ground marks the spot, altho' living residents remember this village well.

It is said that in time as the white people came too close and became too numerous, this village was moved farther south to the place we now know as Onominese. This was after the death of old Kookoosh who lived on the hill where today the farm home of Fred Dechow stands.

There is a legend concerning the moving of Louie Village to Onominese. It shows plainly that old Kookoosh preferred the old village to the new Onominese. After his death, although his body was buried in the new village burying ground, his spirit often haunted the Louie Village vicinity where he had lived.

We are told that one time a farmer who lived in this locality, returning late from the village one night, found his horse stopping stock-still in the middle of the road, raising up on his hind legs, forefeet pawing the air. His driver, suddenly alert and curious, became aware of a cloudlike white figure float weirdly across the road towards the old burying grounds, and on outward to the bluffs where it sailed in midair, out over the lake, disappearing into space.

This was the restless spirit of old Kookoosh haunting the old familiar village where he once lived, and every night wistfully surveying the old burying ground where his spirit had longed to dwell.

Kookoosh's Lament

Kookoosh his restless spirit fly's,
 An apparition white floats before my eyes,
To haunt me o'er these grounds,they say,
 Whose forest paths once trod his way.
"White man,you have blundered here,
 Desecrating hallowed grounds,now fear...
Those wrongs beheld these many nights,
 As I pass about in restless flight!"

As each year the Garthe clan,
 Gather in August from across the land,
To picnic at Peterson Park, and there to talk,
 Of Peterson,and others who once did walk...
of ancestors who roamed this very spot.
 Kookoosh cries out;"My sqaw lies here,where I should
                              dwell,
Must I always flit about the fjell?"

Kookoosh,his long nights vigil spent,
 Cries out in one last lament;
"Within my wigwam,no more fires glow,
 And I am forced to flitter...to and fro,
White man,you have taken land,
 The fish,the game, the forest grand,
Oh Gichie Manitou the Great Creator,
 I implore thy guidance o'er these mischief makers!"

As if in answer to his prayers,
 Ojibwa and Ottawa braves,in death must stare,
At Kookoosh's wild gyrations in mid air,
 As guardians of this hallowed spot,must care,
To see him fly across the bluffs, and shore that lies,
 Before the sun lights morning skies,
Southward to Onominese,his day to sleep,
 O'er Lake Michigan,who's waters are so very deep.

                              M.A.M.

It has been rumored that others, too, passing through this vicinity at night had beheld a cloudlike apparition swishing rapidly by them and disappearing into the night--no doubt the same uneasy spirit haunting its old stamping grounds.

We cannot vouch for the authenticity of this tale for no one can tell us they had actually seen the spectre.

In the early days, William Ring Nose, the old chief of these Indians lived in the vicinity of the present Ole Olson farm and the pioneer remembers his son, Peter Ring Nose as the leader of the Indians of Louie Village.

He wore a small ring in his nose to which was attached a larger ring hanging down over his lips. In his ears, too, were large gold rings giving him the barbaric splendor of a wild chieftain. The pioneer felt, that he, more than any other Indian, resented the intrusion of the white man.

Tom Antoine, whom many of us remember as a very friendly person, was also Indian royalty or near-royalty. His father was sort of a vice chief known as William Neteshing. I don't know why his son took Antoine as a surname.

But there is another interesting story which must concern this same Louie Village and which is more authentic.

Mitchell Gagnon and his sons, Israel, Samuel, George, Marsh and Henry, had migrated from Detroit to the Upper Peninsula where they worked in the smelting of copper. During the slack time of this work, Mitchell and his sons came down into Leelanau County which had recently been put on the market by the government. Here they bought up 500 acres of land. So far as they knew, there was not another white man in the vicinity, tho', according to Miss Craker's history of the early Protestant mission, the Rev. Peter Dougherty, with an Indian guide, had scouted through the region in the year 1838, one year before the founding of Old Mission.

These 500 acres of land which they pre-empted were in the vicinity of Louie Village and included parts of the present farms of Archie Scott, Thos. Roy, Ralph Nelson, and others.

Mitchell Gagnon remained here but a short time and then returned to Detroit. There they found, however, that the smelting business was not so good. It seemed there was an insufficient quantity of ore due to slow lake traffic from the mines, and after three or four years in Detroit, once more, Mitchell Gagnon and his sons turned their faces northward and followed the trail that brought them to their property near Louie Village and, in earnest, they settled down to the hard task of the pioneer home builder. This time when they reached Northport they found several white people, among them Joseph Dame, Geo. N. Smith, John Scott, Thos. Retford, Otis White and others.

Mitchell Gagnon's farm included the western part of the Archie Scott farm. It was here, while plowing with his oxen that the plow hit a hard shining object which, when finally uncovered, proved to be a large ball of copper weighing about two tons. It was a metal familiar to Mr. Gagnon. Perhaps he didn't stop to wonder, as we do today, whence it came, but he knew its value. Laboriously it was loaded into the pioneer wagon, and the oxen hauled it over the rough road to the Bight where Otis White had already built a dock.

Here it was loaded on one of the wood burning steamers, and Mitchell followed it to Detroit. With it he purchased a team of horses which he walked back to his farm on the lake shore, proud in his possession, as he had a reason to be for horses were as yet, scarce.

This story which is not legend, but fact, proves definitely that sometime during the French missionary days of our history, Frenchmen, probably the Jessuits, had stopped, and, perhaps, had lived for a time near Louie Village.

The old copper kettle, so large that the whole carcass of an animal could be cooked at once in it and which was found by the Indians in this vicinity many, many years before, was brought to the blacksmith at Old Mission to be repaired. This was in the early days of the Mission. This interesting episode is described in Ruth Craker's excellent book before mentioned, and which can be read at our Library.

In those early days there were many canoes along our shores, - thin, light craft that varied in size from ten feet to forty and even fifty feet in length. The squaw would sit in front and the Indian in the back with a paddle. Spears were used and many a large sturgeon was caught.

The lake was much higher in those days than now and at Louie Village the water came up to the bluff so there was no beach. Therefore, the Indians drove stakes into the clay bank making sort of a shelf. On these they placed their canoes when not in use.

Reverend Geo ge N. Smith who founded the Indian village
of Waukazooville in 1849, becoming Northport in 1852, re-
established his Old Wing Mission from its former site in
Holland, Michigan to Onominese, lying three miles southwest of
Waukazooville. He started a mission school for the Indian children and a Government Trading Post there. Norman C. Morgan (an
early historian) records that this was home for his mother and
himself from 1866 to the fall of 1869, while his mother taught
school there. The school was located on the high bluffs overlook-
Lake Michigan and surrounded by forest in all directions.

Rev. Smith came over every two weeks to hold religious
services in the little school house, with the Indians coming
from miles atound to hear Reverend Smith expound on the Gospel.
He preached in their own language, and seemed to be the only
white person to be able to hold their undevided attention! When
it came time for hym singing he would get out his tuning fork
to strike the proper pitch for each song they sang. Through these
efforts they sang and prayed as loudly as they cared, pouring
their whole souls and beings into each word of the hym sung!

The first years of Rev. Smith's activities were devoted
towards the upliftment of the Indians, but with the coming of
more whites his scope of usefullness broadened. He even served
several years in the community as the only physician. His services
were given gladly and gratuitously. Before the advent of courts
he invariably was called upon to settle disputes, with his decision
nearly always being accepted without a murmur. Soon after his
establishment of the Onominese Indian School, he was appointed
official interpreter with a Government salary of four hundred
dollars a year. This office he held until his death. He also
started the annual Indian Camp Meetings, the site being about a
mile and one half south of the Indian village of Waukazooville,
where it is still held Indian Methodist Mission Chuches of the
area. As the population of the county increased, so did Rev. Smith's
labors as well.

The Onominese Indian Cemetery

There are approximately 300 hundred graves, mostly unmarked,
in the old cemetery at Onominese. The site of the cemetery lies
within   500 to 600 yards from the edge of a bluffs overlooking Lake Michigan, on rolling hills. No one seems to know
when this cemetery was first started, though it is said that
Indian veterans from the War of Independence with Great Britain
in 1812, have been buried here. There are also veterans from
the Civil War, World War I ,World War II, Korean and the Vetnam
wars buried in this cemetery.

Ownership of the Cemetery

As it is mainly used by the protestant Indians of the
Methodist faith it is said that they should have full control
of the Cemetery, but this has not been so in recent years. Somehow through changes in ownership surrounding the cemetery, the
local Indians and others with ancestors buried here have not
been granted free and easy access to the cemetery. Originally

at the southern boundary of the Cemetery property there had
been a road established,but which was later aband.ned in favor
in favor of a more easy access road.After Emil Carlson,previous
owner of the surrounding property sold to Julian Bowen of Detroit,
in 1964, Indians visiting the Cemetery were then required to
obtain a key to open a padlock to his private road. This proved
very unsatisfactory to the Indians and several well known of
tnis group, including;Jonas Showandosa and Oscar Williams request-
help that something might be still resolved in their lifetime.
With help from Fr. James Gardiner of the St.Wenceslaus Roman
Catholic Parish at Gills Pier, meetings were held with represnt-
ation from veterans organizations, Indian Affairs,and other
sources.This effort in resolving free and easy access was not
resolved, as Mr. Bowen steadfastly felt opening up a road might
lead to vandalism! After Mr. Bowen's death,his wife was agreeable
to leaving the gate open,and that Indians no longer required a
key to get access. The Bowen property has been sold recently to
Richard Firestone, though I do not believe the issue has been
thoroughly resolved.

The Onominese Cemetery has been used primarily by the
Methodist Indian Mission Church,its members of both Chippewa
and Ottawa Indians. Both Jonas Showandosa and Oscar Williams
parents and ancestors are buried in the Onominese Cemetery,
though Jonas requested to be buried with his comrades of the
Spanish American War, at the Oakwood Cemetery in Traverse City.
Jonas served in the Army with the Second Cavalry unit in the
Army of occupation in Cuba.For awhile after the war in Cuba,
he rode horses in the Circus, dressed as an Indian Chief.In
later years he could be counted upon to ride and head the
parade at Memorial Day Ceremonies. Jonas was always concerned
also about the ancient Cemetery at the former Indian village
site of Louisville (Cathead)which has been neglected as well.

Oscar Williams,a painter by trade, was very active in
the affairs of the Methodist Indian Mission Church, and served
on the American Indian Committee,were he was interested in
promoting advanced education for Native American youth. The
following I would like to include as a tribute to both of these
fine men.The article was written by Stephen J.Hutchinson,M.D.,
on a visit to Onominese dated,Aug.29,1876,quote:

" A Sunset at Onominese"

Yesterday while standing on the summit of Onominese bluff
near the Indian Cemetery and the Indian School House,I was fortunate to witness one of the most beautiful Sunsets to behold.
During its last hour it gradually sank beneath the deep waters
of Lake Michigan,in a direction just north of the Manitou's.
During the afternoon it had been cloudy, but suddenly now,in the
late evening the sun burst forth to be viewed in one blaze of
glory,illuminating the horizon and all things with a soft mellow
light of ethereal and wonderful beauty. It set off the forest
trees by shedding its light among the trees and then verging to
the grassy lawn to contrast admirably with the little white
school house,in the center of the scope.Its weird light shed
further abroad and diffused into the atmosphere as though the
Spirits of the Manitou had risen again from the lonely Indian

Cemetery,close by,to bless this spot once more,before ere
taking its final leave. The outline of the shore of the Two
Manitou's were thus distinct as a silver thread. Underneath
the setting sun was observed a dark object, a strange glow
infringing its disk, like a dark strange sail of a departing
ghost,the Ghost of the Great Spirit to leave His world in dark-
ness, and looming as a misty 'Omen', a sign of good things to
come! Further to the south the light distinctly cut across the
shaggy outline of the Sleeping Bear, and as the dusk darkened
into night cast its lurid glare on all things with solemn
grandeur of the moment, deepening and becoming somewhat spectral
and still more impressive. This panorama of light,land,water,
and forest foliage mutually reflecting and mingling, like a
kaleidoscope of nature, reminding me of that equisite verse
of poetry by Milton:" While Shepards watched their flocks by
Night,all seated on the Ground,The Angle of the Lord Came down,
and Glory Shown Around."

        The Indian word Manitou,means something beyond human
capability of understanding. Thus the Indian word Gitchie-man-i-to,
means "Great Spirit" or the equivalent of the Christian word for
"God".Gitchie Man-i-to often is referred to as "Great Creator".
In the Indian legends there is a story of creation where animals
such as the beaver,otter,and a lowly muskrat are sent diving deep
into the waters to bring up soil,and it wasto the muskrat to finally
bring up the first soil to make up"Mother Earth.

        The Indian to my knowledge has always held the two Manitou
Islands as being mysterious in their beliefs as they remained
uninhabited until after the arrival of the first whites and the
need for logging on the islands to fuel the early steamships
traveling down the lake.

The onominese Indian Cemetery

My mother, Inga S. Melkild served as the Leelanau Township librarian, for many years. As librarian she became aware of peoples taste in literature, and had made many acquaintances of those using the library facilities. She related to me the following conversation she had with John Cobb, a native. John's Indian given name was 'Pwahneshing', meaning; "Thunder near the ground!" Back in the mid sixties, John Cobb was then in his mid-seventies. John had been born in the village of Waukazooville, established by Rev. George N. Smith and his band of Ottawa's.

To find out more about the early history of his people, my mother and father (Martin I. Melkild), took John Cobb with them for a drive out to visit the old burial grounds at Onominese, which lies about three miles west of Northport. Arriving at the J.P. Bowen residence, they stopped to obtain permission and a key to open the lock on a gate before taking a winding dirt road to the wooded, hilly cemetery. The name Onominese is said to have been that of an Indian chief who once had lived here, and was said to have come from the Wisconsin shores.

Arriving first to the oldest part of the cemetery, John pointed to the spot where Old Kookoosh was buried, his grave lying north and south, not like that in former times when no importance was made to direction in which the body should lie! It is a legend that Old Kookoosh's spirit leaves his grave to visit the grave of his squaw buried near Peterson Park, and where he would rather dwell! John Cobb, then remarked; "Anyway, all full here-tight as can be!" We then stumble up the steep hillside and come to a newer section of the cemetery. On thse graves, were many markers of wood, with some names neatly inscribed, while others had been defaced by time and weather. Amongst them were a scattering of headstones marking the resting spot of men who had fought for their country. Scouts who had served in the Revolutionary War, the Civil War, World War I and II, and the Korean War. Walking amongst the graves we made out the following names; George Ashkebug Co. K 1st Mich. S.S., Alex Wahsaquom 91st Div., Daniel and Angelina Wayashi, Thomas Redbird, Edward Hall Prvt, 105 Inf., Joseph Wanageshik, W.W.II.

In asking John, about the early burial customs of his people, John replied; "When a man of the tribe died, usually some apparatus used by him in hunting or fishing was buried with him. For a wamon, it was something she had worked with during her life, such as a clay dish, beads, or needles she had sewn with. If a child, it was usually a toy to play with that it had loved.

Before coffins were used, the body was wrapped in sheets of soft skins, covered outside by long strips of birch bark, and then tied with raw hide strings. In most cases little huts made from birch bark or elm bark covered the grave, where little gifts of food were often left for the departed. As to their destination after death, all Indians believed they were going to the "Happy Hunting Grounds", that there they would meet "Gitchie Manito", their God and Great Creator of us all! Here all good Indians would live peacefully, each in his own wigwam, with his own garden patch - but a bad Indian would be put into a corner by himself, away from others, and looked upon with contempt, with no one to associate with!

In inquiring why as to the graves in the Indian Cemetery at Peshawbestown were decorated with wreaths and colored paper flowers, and draped over the crosses,John said; "It is the custom to decorate the graves in the late summer, it being the belief that on November 1st spirits of the dead came back to their last resting place on earth, to see if they had been taken care of. Relatives of the departed would celabrate at this time, and as they feasted broke off pieces of food, especially that which the departed had liked in life. This portion was then placed into the burning fire, and sometimes a spoonful of spirits (fire water) was thrown in for those departed who had a weakness for it in life. So one must make it agreeable for their unseen guests, during the once a years visit back home!"

As my parents then left the cemetery and walked westward towards the bluffs which rises several hundred feet above Lake Michigan's shoreline, one cannot but remark about the beautiful view of North and South Manitou Islands to the west, and the Fox Islands in the north. Southward is the promontary of Port Onieda jutting into the lake, and still further southward is the promontory of Sleeping Bear. It being told that in early times when Indians traveled southward down Lake Michigan on their annual journey to their winter hunting camps, they would stop to pay homage to "Gitchie Manito,the Great Creator", leaving little gifts of food offerings,as well!

Now while gazing out over the Lake towards the Manitou's, John Cobb told the story about his grandparents who with a party of Indians had made a trip to North Manitou Island in their canoes. Upon their arrival at the shorethey were met by four large hens and one large rooster, coming from out of the woods. The party tried creeping stealthily forward to catch them,but just as suddenly they vanishedbefore their eyes. Indian being naturally superstitious,this included, took fright and hastened back to the mainland. At this time in history there were no known settlers living on the island.The Manitou Islands have always held some spell of enchantment over the native Indians. Manitou- denotes both good and bad;South Manitou is good account of its protective harbor and austral winds,while North Manitou, bad , in a boreal sense, cold chilly and without a safe harbor.

Before leaving Onominese ,John Cobb pointed to where the Indian Government School building had once stood, and where as a boy he had gone to school.Nothing now remains but a scattered stone pile, or where other buildings of the village once stood. Near by was the spring which still flowed from its clay bank, its clear cool waters the only reminder of a past habitation of Onominese

Chapter VII.
Stories As Told By Charles E. Garthe

Uncle Issac Garthe and Chris Blacken built a boat which was used in fishing off the beach which is now Peterson Park. It was stolen and reported to be on Manitou Island. A group of neighborhood men went over to the island to recover it, but it seems that the thief was reluctant to give it up. But as the group had brought along some convincing baseball sized clubs they were able to get the boat back with only one of the group. a man by the name of "Buss" being slightly hurt!

Oscar Peterson said that when the families came from Norway and while crossing the Ocean, different parties took turns in the galley of the ship. One day Chris Blacken had a fire going in galley to boil some potatoes and a huge wave came over the ship, slamming open the door to the galley and in shloshing about lifted the lids of the stove.

The first Lutheran Church services were said to be held at the Chris Blacken home which stood on Nelson road. Later Chris became Chief of Police for Traverse City. Then son John became Chief and still later his grandson Charlie Woodrow was Chief for many years.

Uncle Hans came from Norland, Norway and had a different Norwegian dialect than the rest of us, so we tried to mimic his speech. His son Oscar said when his father would sail with a fishing crew as far out as the Lofoten Islands in his younger days, that he would have to take his own food consisting of fish balls and flat bread or hard tack in his lunch box. After a number of days at sea the fish balls and the hard tack would become as hard as golf balls and the flat bread or hard tack would shatter like glass when bitten into. Hans Peterson was said to never have cavities in his teeth. Olaf Eiken, who once stayed at the Peterson"s and helped on the farm while going to school said that Hans would occasionally take a common file and file them down to suit himself. This made Olaf Eiken shudder. In those early days Hans would test the temper of an axe by biting it. Incidently my own father, Steiner, teeth were perfect to the end of his life and I remember him telling about a man named "Nigger Brown", who was a barber in Northport, who would select the hardest shelled nuts to be found and dad would crack them with his teeth.

Once when the Peterson children were small Hans stepped into something before coming into the house that smelled pretty bad, and said;"De stinker so forbana folk connat comme I husset!" Another morning after having dne chores in the barn,,uncle Hans complained,"My goodnesssakes Hertie(his Wife),"her en klokken 9 ennu er ikke Breakfast ready?"

I remember hearing about false lights being rigged so that ships would go aground at the islands in the early days, though this might not be the case I wish to tell about. One time with Jean and our family we held a picnic at Peterson Park along with my brotherin-law Lawernce Foley and Oscar Peterson. Oscar then told us about his father being hired by a party in Northport and ther- going to South Fox Island where they toiled unloading a shipload of salt pork. They filled every building there that

availlable with the barrels of salt pork. There must have
been something not quite right because after they got back
to Northport Hans spent a good half day in a room that was
blue with smoke with the party they had worked for.It was
rmored that a family living at Harbor Springs were selling
salt pork all along the coast of western Michigan.

A number of newcomers spent some time working for dad
on the farm as they were earning their keep to a new way of
life in America.One of these was John Hummelstad who later
settled near Gills Pier.One day dad gave John a hoe to hoe
the corn.At first it seems he was unfamiliar with the hoe and
was afraid he would break it as he had only been familiar with
a grub hoe.At noon after coming in for lunch,he asked,"what
were the weeds with the large leaves growing like a vine"?
Of course these were pumpkins which we always planted along
with the corn,He had been hoeing them all out!

Lars and Hans Sogge were two other men who spent some
time working on the farm.Hans was a favorite of Seth and
Christine.Lars became a merchant in Suttons Bay and Otto Bahle
married his daughter.

The Larson s had a nice farm a mile south of our farm.
The grandparents Ole Moe and his wife lived with them.Ole was
short and stout and his wife still stouter and never seemed
to bear a smile.One Saturday afternoon after Ole took off the
wheels on the buggy and applied miks axle grease they set off
for town,his wife had loaded the crocks of butter and a basket
of eggs to do the usual Saturday trading .When Mrs. Moe came
into the store at Northport her hat was crumpled with its
one feather sticking off at an angle. There were eggs and dirt
all over her clothes.The clerk asked her in astonishment what
had happened? Without the least sign of a smile she said;"Oh
Ole mine he forgot to screw the wheels behind!"

I have a song book printed in Norwegian from Christiana,
Norway,which is now called Oslo with my name Charles Garthe and
date being 21,Nov.1909 printed in gold print on its cover.This
may have been the last class or near the last class that were
to beconfirmed in the Lutheran Church in Norwegian.At this time
there were two Norwegian Churches in Northport.Dad was the
"klokker" of the Synod Church and uncle Hans Peterso "klokker"
at the Conference Church.The "klokker" or kanter would lead
the singing after the opening services.In the earlier days this
was done without any organ or other instrument to help them
with the right pitch.They said that Uncle Hans stoppedin to the
Methodist Church one Saturday night while Deacon Dame was in
the process of building.Hans made the rafters ring with his loud
Amen's.He had a strong voice,but possibly a nip of brandy to
help out as well.

I remember the day that news arrived that Norway got it's
independence from Sweden the 17th of May.There was sort of an
ill feeling between the Norwegians and the Swedes,perhaps because
the Swedes felt they were more sophisticated.It was about 60
years before I knew how Norway got it's independence.it seems
that the Swedish Army was massed and equipped to cross the line.

It seems as the troups were lined up for Roll Call,pieces of

paper began falling to the ground in front of each squad
or near by.When these were picked up the thousands of papers
were read;"Don't fight the Norwegians,and you will have a
lifelong friend instead of a lifelong enemy." I knew this to
true as I heard this from a soldier in the Swedish army
who was in the ranks at this time.

We can see now that the Nowegians are peace lovers and
here note that Norway's Trigve Lee was Secretary of the United
nations and then Dag Hammershol was also Secretary of the
United Nations.

My dad Steiner Garthe and Henning Waagbo each bought two
fourties of land and then traded a forty in order that each
of their properties were closer together,making each 80 acres.
There was a small clearing made by the Indian's long ago,and
and a few seedling apple trees near the bluffs.When dad first
settled having as yet not married, he then cut hay in this clear
and after making this into a sack covered it with some boards
then dug himself a hole into it to form a place for him to sleep.
He found a spring part way down the bluffs,and scooped out a
hole and dipped out his water to drink. He then built his first
log cabin just northwest of the present house. I remember him
telling me of his telling me of having a pet pig that he let
run loose and would follow him when he went to cut wood.At that
time it would eat beach nuts and root for other food.But though
it became firm and sleek it died.

The Henning land is what became the Talgo property and
uncle Jake Waagbo got the north of that property.One day Henning
asked the nearby pioneers for some help to build a shelter.He
had found a very large tree which had fallen down and used this
to be one side of the house.With extra help they completed the
other three walls,put on a roof and by night time the house was
ready for him to live in!

Herman Waagbo was born at Northport Dec.15,1888.He
graduated from Michigan Agric.College,East Lansing in 1913 His
fatherJacob Waagbo had farmed the land for forty years the best
he knew how and had finally declared it to be useless.After
Herman returned from college having learned new methods of
farming,by plowing under ten acres and again reseeding in the
like amount of acreage per year after,produced a fine yield of
250 bushels of certified seed potatoes per acre on top of the
alfalfa sod.One year when other farmers hay crops went bad,and
were without feed for their cattle,Herman Waagbo had alfalfa to
sell which he sold to the whole neighborhood.All farmers suddenly discovered that Herman's education and new methods had paid
him well and they likewise sowed alfalfa for cover crops.

Herman Waagbo kept forty acres into alfalfa and using a
four year rotation,was able to plow under ten acres a year,which
he put into ten acres of certified seed potatoes each year.He
thus proved that soil can be brought back into production!

Herman Waagbo remained a bachelor, active in civic affairs
and in his church (Bethany Lutheran). He helped out the youth
groups by picking them up with his car and transporting them
to the Luther League functions.

He often picked up the neighbor boys in his model T Ford
and drove them to Kehl Lake for an early swim before the
waters of Lake Michigan or the Bay had warmed.

Herman probably had the neatest work shop in   all of
Leelanau County, and before the advent of 'REA' he had installed a wind generator to produce electricity to power and
light his farm buildings.

The Sinking Of The George Rogers

The Steam Tug George Rogers out of Cheboygan, Michigan,
while on her way down the Lake, caught fire. The crew were
unable to put out the fire, and were then forced to head in
to shore where she sank off the Garthe Bluffs, on August 28,
1913. Its bones can still be seen today. The wet crew made
there way up the steep trail to the Garthe farm where they
were warmly received, fed and spent the night before heading
back home to Cheboygan the next day. Ray Thomas who lived
and farmed adjacent to the Garthe and Waagbo farm relates
the following events, I quote: "George Abbott who had a fish
tug at Northport, came around to the wreck and salvaged parts
and the tow cables from the wreck. Fred Baumberger who was in
need of a boiler for a shingle mill, decided to salvage the
boiler. He then purchased the tow cables from George Abbott,
and after freeing the boiler from the wreck hitched three
teams of horses to it, and managed to skid it ashore. He then
waited until the ice on thelake was sufficiently thick to
haul the boiler on a logging sled to what is now called peterson Park. When they had traveled about a half mile, the rear
bobs of the sled broke through the ice, and further salvage
operations were abandoned. Fred Baumberger having expended
upwards of $1,000, in expenses in hiring his cousin Rufus
Ranger as teamster, and having to shoe the three teams of
horses with extra long cleats(to get extra grip on the ice)
   by blacksmith, Oscar Kitchen.

Lars Lee, nephew of Herman Waagbo remembers hearing
how thetugs were cut to save the horses from drowning. He
and many other neighbor boys would swim out to the boiler
   and on a clear still day one could still see runners
of the sled under the boiler along with the cut tugs.

In researching further on the George Rogers I found
out the tug was built in Toledo, Ohio in 1889 by H. J. Trout.
She measured 77.3 x 18.3 ft. She weighed 64 gross tons-33
net tons. Engine-Fore and aft compound steam engine. Cylinders:
12 inx22 in.x 18 in.stroke. Fire boiler measured: 16.25 x11ft.
She had a number of owners, and at the time of her sinking
was owned by the Carow Towing Company, Cheboygan, Michigan .
The following letter was received by Seth Garthe.

At the time of my conversation about the "George Rogers",
Ray Thomas was nighty nine years of age and living by himself
on the old Nels Blacken farm near Peterson Park,but has since
passed away.He went on to tell meabout the early fishing days
at Peterson Park,saying;"There had been a shop across the
road from the Blacken place,near where the the present Fox
View Estates are today.At this shop they built small wooden
kegs.The fishermen would salt their catch in these kegs and
then bury them in the sand in order to escape the game wardens
eye.When the season they would sell their hidden kegs of fish."
He also said;:That "Black Fin" fish,a soft fleshed fish,was an
excellent fish for smoking,but they can no longer be found in
the Great Lakes,as they have been all fished out."

Picture circa. 1914, wreck of the steam tug George Rogers.
Left to right, brothers James, Charles and Seth Garthe.

```
          CAROW  TOWING  COMPANY
          Complete Towing and Lighterage
                    Facilities

Tug BOB STEPHENSON
    -------
Tug GEO. ROGERS

    Steam Stearing
    Steam Towing Machine
    Gasoline Tender


                    CHEBOYGAN, MICH.
                        Aug. 30, 1913

Mr. Seth Garthe,
        North Port, Mich.

Dear Sir:

     The Captain and Crew of the tug "Geo. Rogers"
arrived here this morning and reported the very kind
and generous treatment received at your hands after
meeting with disaster night before last and they and
Carow Towing Co. wish to express our appreciation and
gratitude.

     We would also like to ask you as a further favor to
please take care of the life boat which the boys
pulled up on the beach and if possible prevent anything
being taken or molested on or about the wreck of the
"Rogers" until we can get things straightened around.

     Again thanking you, wish to remain,


                    Yours truly,



                    O. B. Martin
```

In further conversation,Ray Thomas stated that his brother Halbert Thomas had attended the Benzonia Academy and then went on to the University of Michigan School of Dentistry. His first practice in dentistry was in the building at Northport that later was used by Peter Eiken for a bakery.Halbert Thomas,D.D.S. later moved his practice to Suttons Bay.

Ray went on to tell how their farm was surrounded by many Norwegians,and how hard it was to get on the telephone (a party line), as it was continually monopolized by the Norske women, who prattled on in endless conversation,most of the time in their native tongue,telling about their favorite recipies or other bits of gossip of the day! He also related that the following relatives had inherited monies from the estate of a great uncle Probst in New York State and with these funds came to purchase lands and settle in Leelanau: Truman Kilcherman,Annette Kilcherman,Robert Thomas,Robert Probst, Fred Baumberger,and Charlie Rufli.

The Nels Blacken - Peter Eiken Fish Shanty
at Peterson Park

It seems that the steamer,Joseph H.Hurd,a 592 ton wooden vessel,171 feet in length,built in Detroit in 1869, was destined to a life of danger,and narrow escapes.The Petoskey paper, Northern Independent,writes on Friday,May 10,1895;quote;The Cayuga,built in Cleveland in 1889,at a cost of $175,000.00, with a steel hull,290 feet in length,41 feet wide and 1939 net tons had left Chicago the day before with a full load of flour and merchandise bound for Buffalo.

The two steamers,the Joseph H.Hurd and Cayuga,neared each other just south of the Skilligalee Light off Charlevoix, the wind was abeam and in the fog all sounds were distorted. Although both vessels had been blowing their whistles at regular intervals,there was some misunderstanding of passing singals and the two ships collided at full speed. With the impact of the Hurd stoving into the cargo hold of the Cayuga about 12 feet.The impact had sheared the bow completely off the Hurd, but she still remained afloat. The Cayuga was in much worse condition and begain to sink. The crew of the Cayuga were taken off onto the Hurd and then the Hurd made a gallant attempt to shore,and finally reaching the beach near Harbor Springs. It seems that the morning after this mishap a strange sight greet- ed the people who had come down to see the wreck. Little Grand Traverse Bay looked like it had become a giant mixing bowl. The flour from the Cayuga had mixed with water and incoming waves kept washing great chunks of dough onto the beach!. Nearby Indians were excitedly running around gathering up the dough which was starting to bake by the warmth of the sun. Carrying the dough away in buckets and baskets to their homes, shouting to any and all,"Heap plenty bread, Injun no have to work now!" So like the lighthouse keeper on South Fox said; "Throwing bread upon the waters!"

Another story told to Charles by his father,about an early 'hooker' or trading schooner which had come into the harbor at Northport.One of the merchants had a considerable amount of butter which had turned rancid and he was unable to sell,as back in those days there was'nt much refrigeration, this being a frequent occurrence during those hot days of summer. The 'Hooker'Captain promptly bought all of this rancid butter at a bargain price.Taking it aboard his ship he then set to work washing it clean after placing it on the canvas deck,and then reworking the mass of butter in a crude mortar box he had made,with a garden hoe;and perhaps adding a bit more of season- ing to it!He then refilled the crocks and sold it at the next port of call! Such were the workings of business deals in the "good old days!"

The Missing Son

George,one of the sons of Mitchell Gagnon was said to have had twenty four children. Large families on a farm was a common occurance in the early days,and it was deemed to be essential and profitable! The Gagnon's were having quite a time in keeping track of their cattle, as clearings where they grazed were not yet fenced in, which led to there straying. One evening son Laurence was sent to fetch the cows for milking. When it became dark, and Laurence and the cows had not yet returned home, another son was sent to find them and soon brought them home.

Laurence did not show up that evening,or in the morning. The family was not too much disturbed,as usually with a large family, one child amongst twenty four was not to br missed! But inquiries were soon made to the nearest neighbors of Laurence's whereabouts, without any results. It was then assumed that something violent might have taken place with him, such as an encounter with a bear!

Seven years later the Gagnon's received a card post-marked Chicago. The first line,read; "Did the cows get home?" Then went on to relate of the events of the day when Laurence had gone to fetch the cows,and telling of how he had made the acquaintance of several sailors who were off a schooner which had anchored off what is now called "Peterson Park" and at that time being the Indian settlement called Louisville. The schooner's captain had stopped to barter with the Indians there. The sailors had convinced Laurence about an adventurous life in the big city of Chicago,where they were headed, and any-thing seemed better to Laurence than tending cows to Laurence!

Note: AN Oscar Peterson
story. M.A.M

Sunken Treasures Off Leelanau

Who isn't interested in stories of sunken treasure?

Two early Northport men, george Bigelow and Al Voice remember
when a two or three masted schooner sank over the shoals two
miles west of Cathead, in the early fifties. In her hold lies
280 casks of whiskey , with each caskbeing 50 gallons. Tom Haynes
who lived near Cathead Bay is said to have removed the schooners
spars during the winter when the ice had froze to withstand any
great weight. The spars of fine pine were used in making shingles.

Walter Voice, the son of Al Voice also recalls of another sail-
vessel which lies northeast of Cathead and three miles due west
of Grand Traverse Light, in 60 to 70 fathoms.

The sinking of the Westmoreland

Frank Fisher arrived as a boy to Glen Arborwith his parents
from Wisconsin to homestead prperty near Sleeping Bear on Aug.8th
1854, four months prior to the sinking of the Westmoreland. He was
told of her sinking by Paul Pelky one of the crew suvivors aboard
the Westmoreland.

The Westmoreland an earlysteamer on the lakes had run into
a terrible northwest storm out of Chicago, which swept all cargo
off her decks and filling her fire hold below with water. Capt.
Henry Dorsey tried to seek shelter of the harbor at South Manitou
Island, but with her firehold and engines flooded, began to drift
northeastward into Platte Bay. Captain Dosey along with his crew
tried to arouse the 17 lumberjacks aboard who had begun a drunken
party soon after leaving Chicago. This proved to be of avail and
the Captain was forced to leave them when launchingthe ships
yaul. The Westmoreland sank approximately five and one half to six
miles off Platte River Bay. It is reported the Westmoreland carried
aboard a shipment of $10,000.00 in gold and other valuables in
her safe. Securely battened in her hold lies 2,800 casks of ripe
whiskey. The Westmoreland was a wooden hulled propeller, 160 feet
in length. She had cast her hauser in Chicago on Dec.4, 1854

The Francisco Morazon

On Dec.8,1960, the Francisco Morazon, an Liberian freighter
254 feet in length and 2000 tons was up bound frm Chicago bound
for Rotterdam. Her Captain was 26 year old Eduardo Trivizas, native
of the Greek Island of Corfu. Along with his wife, Anastasia, who
was expecting a child was aboard. The Captain became off course
and grounded on rocks off the southwest shore of South Manitou.

Three Coast Guard shipd, the Mackinaw, Mesquite, and the Sun-
dew, went to aid of the disabled freighter, but were unable to
free her from the rocks.

Much of the cargo was of canned chicken, with George Grovner
of Leland working under an oral agreement withPete Jurica and
Mercie Day, operators of the Lake Michigan Hardwood Company contract-
ing to remove the cargo to Leland. She alsocarried acargo of chem-
ical products, machinery, lard, and hides besides the chicken. It was
rumored that there was an abundance of canned chicken floating all
the county!

Early Fishing

Hans Peterson most likely made the selection for his farm and home site by its proximity to the good fishing grounds, having been known by the early Indians of Cathead village. Here it has been said that in earlier days when the water level was much higher than today, there were no beaches and the Indian drove stakes into the clay bank to form a shelf on which to place their light birch bark canoes. In those early times there schools of sturgeon easily speared along the shore.

The first white fisherman built shanties below the bluffs for their fishing gear, storage, and a place to sleep. Cribs were placed out the lake and filled with stone to form a dock. A stone bob pulled by a horse was used in carrying the fish boxes up the trail. In these early days the fish were packed in boxes with salt or in kegs for transportation to markets like Chicago, by schooners or(Hookers). Later fish shipped from North- port were packed in ice and shipped by rail and steamships of theNorthern Transit C..

Feb.24,1891, it was reported that Will Redford and Ed Middleton of Northport took 1400 pounds of fish, which was con- sidered a normal catch. At the turn of the century, the fishing fleet had increased to five commercial docks. Shipping by water was also needed for the rising fruit industry as reported by the Enterprise, a weekly paper. In September 1880, about 500 bushels of apples and peaches had been sent to Chicago on the ship, Fountain City. The fruit then sold on the market as high as $2.00 a bushel. But the fruit farmer was often placed in a precarious position by the stock brokers in the big city, who took considerable amounts from his profit as being spoilage, often with out just cause!

As steamship traffic increased a whole new industry began to flourish, as tourists arrived homes began opening to furnish room and board. By the turn of the century the fishing industry at Northport supported as many as sixteen fish tugs and fifty in this employment.

Joseph Dame was deputy collector for the port of Northport (1856-66) and from his day book we have secured the list of boats (propellers) that made this port.

LIST OF PROPELLERS

The "Sunny side" - first boat to run on the Bay in summer of 1864-65. Owned by Hannah Lay & Co. with Capt. Johnson, father of Capt. George Johnson of Traverse City, its master. It foundered in a storm off Charlevoix.

The "Allegan" first boat to run between Traverse City and Chicago - a weekly route - until replaced by "City of Traverse".

Wrecks: Sardinia, loaded with salt
          (?) Limes, loaded with car sills
It is said the crew had their clothes stolen by the natives.

The City of Buffalo] Called at the Bight at the time the
The City of Richmond] Woolsey's came

The Oneida - Capt. Stewart - Capt. Miller
The Mohawk - Capt. T.W. Steele
City of Traverse - Capt. Ball - Capt. Welch
St. Louis - Capt. N. Woodworth (at the Bight)
City of Chicago - Capt. James Welch
The Badger State - Capt. Gibaud
The B.F. Wade - Capt. C.B. Goldsmith
The City of Boston - Captain's name obliterated.
The Bristol - Capt. Boyd
The Plymouth - Capt. Fairbanks
The Forest Queen - Capt. Corrigan
The City of New York - Capt. Chadwick.
      Later disabled and towed (1856) into port by the City
      of Madison - Capt. Price.
The Evergreen - Capt. Conelon
The Gelena - Capt. Penny
The Wabash - Captain's name obliterated.
The Sun - Capt. Jones
Queen of the Lakes -
The Free State - Capt. S. N. Atwood
The Bradburry - Capt. Hunt
The Potomac - Capt. Carlisle
The Mayflower - (1866) Capt. Palmer - Capt. Drake
The Allegheny - Capt. Bayington
The Montgomery - Capt. Gillis
The Idaho - Capt. Goldsmith - Capt. Conkey
The Fountain City - Capt. Dodge
The Van Ralte - Capt. Dodge
The Winslow -
The Dean Richmond - Capt. Bennet
The Winona - Capt. Collins
The Geo. P. Savage - Capt. Smith
The City of Grand Rapids - Capt. Oscar Wilbur

The Champlain - Capt. Casey
    Burned off Charlevoix - Rebuilt and called The City of
    Charlevoix - Capt. Knucken
        Rebuilt and called - The Kansas
The Lawrence - Capt. Boyd
The Vernon - lost off Leland or near Cat Head
The Cummings - Capt. Robinson
The Clarabel - Capt. Wilbun
The Mermaid - Capt. Dave Perran
The Onekema - Capt. Emery
The Puritan -
The Faxton - Capt. Will Franklin
The Missouri - Capt. Knucken - Capt. Johnson
Alice M. Gill - Capt. Robinson - Capt. Will Franklin
The Manitou - Capt. Franklin -Capt. Johnson
Carferry M.M.&N. #1 - Capt. Robertson

The Onekewin   ]   Between Northport and Northport Point
The Dorothy K.]   I.L. Dame
The Venus   ]

The Cresent - Capt. Parrish - Capt. Webb
The Columbia - Capt. Young

CHAPTER IX.

A REMINISCENT SKETCH BOOK

To those descendants of our early
pioneers who still love the land
and cherish its frontier traditions,
these sketches are humbly dedicated

        Maret Garthe
        Winifred Hutchinson Schroeder
        Alice Gill Scott
            Committee

We learn from a Centennial address given by Judge Hatch of Traverse City, July 4, 1876, that Joseph Dame landed at Old Mission Sept. 18, 1841, superseding John M. Johnson as Indian farmer sent by the government.

The next year Mr. Dame sowed the first wheat in this region. He raised a good crop, but there was no mill. He raised this grain every year thereafter and in time had enough to take to the mill--not to the Hannah and Lay Mill, for Mr. Hannah had not seen the Grand Traverse Region at this time--but to Green Bay! We think--how they must have appreciated a slice of white bread!

Mr. Dame remained at Old Mission for three years when he moved to Wisconsin on account of his family's health. He remained there seven years. He returned about 1851 as far as the North Manitou Islands and a fish boat took him to the mainland and the vicinity of what is now Northport. Here he found Rev. G. N. Smith and his Indians. Here, too, he found a good harbor.

In company with a man named Merrill he sent to the land office at Ionia and entered 30 acres of land. The next winter with Indian help he built a wharf.

Mr. Smith, who was then here was, no doubt, the first white settler. Small pox had driven him and his Indians from their mission at Allegan and in company with James McLaughlin, he had reached Northport vicinity.

James McLaughlin, assisted by the whole community, had erected the first log dwelling.

Mr. Dame was very much pleased with the region and decided to write it up. He sent a glowing description of the Grand Traverse region in a letter to the New York Tribune. It was published in March.

The nearest post office was at Old Mission with mail about once a month. Mr. Dame went to the post office for the first mail following the publication of his letter and received 64 inquiries. The next month he received 44 more, and on each subsequent mail day many more. The country was ready and immigration had begun in earnest. Soon a village made its appearance and plans had to be made here. Mr. Smith laid out Waukazooville in 1849 and Deacon Dame laid out Northport in 1852 with Nagonaby street, the town line, between them.

This early twin-town arrangement, no doubt, accounted for the jog in the street where Waukazoo Street joins Nagonaby and continues past Mervau's drug store as Mill Street.

Waukazooville was annexed to Northport and the name Northport remained.

As early as 1853-54 Deacon Dame started a dock on the site of the present Cherry Home dock. It was finished in 1855 by H. O. Rose, who took in as his business partner Amos Fox and thus began the pioneer establishment of Fox and Rose.

They were the first dock owners on Grand Traverse Bay where steamers, or propellers, as they were called, could land. Fuel for lake steamers at that time was cordwood and from the present site of Cook's Market and east to the shore were piles of cord-wood, acres of them, eight feet high, used by these ever increasing steamboats, and over this dock was shipped, annually, from 20 to 50 thousand cords of wood.

Another dock built by Campbell and Goodrich, sometimes called the Union Dock, was located near the foot of Main Street, the old spiles of which can be seen yet. Here, too, cord wood made an active business.

Later when land had been cleared and farmsteads started, the cord wood business decreased and schooners made their appearance - two, three, and sometimes four-masted ships riding in majestically to take on a cargo of potatoes which became the major crop of the erstwhile woodchopper, a crop that yielded well on the fertile soil of new land and still continues as a staple crop.

But in 1855 there was not a frame house in our village. The first complete frame house was built by Mr. Thomas for Mr. Woodruff in 1856. That year saw the completion of Mr. Voice's saw mill, too. This mill, through the early years, supplied the lumber for the early homes in the village and surrounding country.

Thus, with a mill to supply building material other frame houses began to appear among the log houses and the '60s became an era of homebuilding.

Mr. Moffatt built the C. S. Nelson house about 1859 or '60. Wm. Voice built the house now occupied by Ernest Cook in 1858. This was the Voice home where Abbie Voice Morgan was born.

The building which houses the library was the Burbeck house. Mr. Burbeck, one of the early merchants built the one time Gill's store which burned to the ground about 1906 or '07. The original Gill store stood on the corner of Nagonaby and Mill Streets where we now have the Dame and Son building. When Mr. Gill moved to the Steele drug store at the foot of Main Street before he purchased the Burbeck store, this building was moved back to the creek and remodeled into a dwelling house which was occupied by Frank Calhoun for a number of years. More recently this same building has been moved to Sixth Street and at the present writing is occupied by Arthur Dalzell and family.

Main Street was well named for it was a busy thoroughfare. At its foot was the Union Dock and opposite the Effie Leslie house stood Sol Steel's drug store which was occupied by William Gill until he bought the Burbeck store as above stated, and Mr. Burbeck moved to Harbor Spring.

Mr. Richard Thomas has given us some reminiscences that throw some light on the ways and means of those early days. Necessity, always the mother of invention, provides a way.

Fences were used to fence in and protect the crops only and live stock, cattle, horses and hogs, ran wild through the woods and were rounded up at night by the younger members of the family. Wild-cats and bears were seen occasionally, as well as numerous porcupines, rabbits, woodchucks, etc.

Mr. Thomas tells that often it grew dark before the cattle were located and then he would catch firm hold of the tail of one of the cows and let her guide him home. With roads few and poor and trails none too numerous it was not an easy thing for a child with a flock of cattle to find the way home through the woods after dark. If one lived near the shore it was easier for he could follow the beach.

When the Thomas family came in 1856 they brought with them seven barrels of flour but the spring of '57 saw very little left for much had been lent to neighbors who had none at all. Indians supplied them with fish every week. They had no scales to weigh them and needed none--one fish, regardless of size was, sometimes five cents sometimes ten cents depending upon good or poor fishing, or fisherman's luck.

In summer wild blackberries, raspberries and strawberries grew in abundance where the timber had been cut off and scores of people would be picking together.

The first mill at Northport was built by William Voice. It was a small mill and used to cut lumber for local consumption. It was located on the present dam and was run by water power. Robert Lee bought this mill and to it added a grist mill. He also built the flume.

Mr. Lee also bought the house now owned by Willard Hall. This had been a hotel run by a Mr. Jones. Mr. Sol Steele had built this house.

Mr. Voice's broom-handle factory stood on the present O. K. Meat Market site. Below this on the creek, the old Exchange Hotel was purchased by Mr. Royce who had married Al. Voice's sister. It was converted into a fish cannery run by Kennedy and McFee.

Campbell and Goodrich had built the house now occupied by the Roy Steeles. It is interesting to know that Mr. Campbell married Libby Ingalls whose parents lived at Ingalls Bay near Omena, Libby Ingalls taught at the Bight and boarded round as was the custom. Her brothers and sisters attended the Bight school, while she taught there, making the trip with horses every day during the school year, a distance of about nine miles!

William Woolsey had a wagon shop where Arthur Hubele's restaurant now stands.

The George Purkiss house, now occupied by Mr. Stafford and family, is also an old house built by Mr. Putt, a friend of William Gill.

The first U. S. Coastal Survey of Grand Traverse Bay was made in 1861. Their camp was established where the Telgard shipyard is now located. Wooden towers were built every half mile and a trail was cut from the high sand hill west of Cat

Head to Seven Pines on the Bay to get vision for establishing
a base line.
     The officer in charge of this survey became General Meade
of Civil War renown. This was about the time the beginnings
of our village were being laid.

The Passenger Pigeon

One of the extraordinary phenomenon of nature in connection with the development of this part of Michigan was the unnumbered flocks of wild pigeons that frequented this section in the early days, and then, their <u>sudden</u> and <u>complete</u> disappearance in 1881.

In the spring they began, flying very high toward the Northwest over the lake, a little before the snow went off. As the snow disappeared they began to alight for feeding.

A person who remembers them well and helped to catch them says "It is almost impossible to describe them. They came in such unbelievable numbers!"

He remembers that it would take some flocks two hours to pass by the sun--flocks that were at least five miles wide, and some say, a hundred miles long! Allowing one square yard to a bird one could figure out the approximate number in such a flock.

The nearest nesting places were at Cedar Run, Petoskey and Mullet Lake but there were many feeding places.

Feeding beds were made in the woods by clearing away all rubbish that might tangle the nets. Spring nets were about 20 ft. by 40 ft., tied on a rope 12 ft. X 30 ft., and would make sort of a bag when trapped.

When the birds were trapped, the trappers, with crates, would get under the net and put the birds in these crates which held about six dozen. They were sold in the village, one dollar being the usual price for a six dozen crate.

They were then transferred to a larger crate or coop about 16x16x4 ft. and held until shipment to Chicago--usually to a Col. Bond who was at that time president of the Chicago Shooting Club, and the unhappy birds were used by sportsmen for trap shooting.

At one time 4000 doz. were cooped in crates ready for shipment from our village alone.

Capt. Kirkland, who was from Connecticut, was in command of one of the boats that handled this sort of freight and he, no doubt, did some advertising of his own for this sport attracted many people to this community at this time.

But not all the pigeons were shipped alive. Catchers would go to the nesting places--the nearest one being Cedar Run. Before they were quite full size the heavy squabs would fall from their nests and the parent birds would feed them on the ground. So dogs were trained to catch the squabs which were then killed and iced for shipment.

Mr. C. I. Wrisley tells of his experience as a boy when he was allowed to go to Cedar Run with Mr. Walt Wilson, father of Miss Emma Wilson. Mr. Wilson who was a blacksmith made the pincers, or tongs, with which the birds were killed.

Mr. Wrisley, a mere boy at the time, was allowed to go on condition they would not stop at Suttons Bay where they had the measles. But when they got to Meberts", they stopped, and Mr. Mebert said, "Come in and see my boy Henry." They went in. Henry had the measles! However Charles suffered no ill consequences from the exposure and they went on to Traverse

City, then on to Cedar Run.

Charlie had always "had a way" with horses and, even when a small boy, was a good teamster. That was the reason he was allowed to drive the team that hauled the squabs by the wagon box, like potatoes, to Traverse City. Mr. John A. Jackson bought and packed for all the catchers that season. It was an important and lucrative business!

Mr. Wrisley also tells another interesting episode of his youth.

The Wrisleys were among those who came here for the pigeon shooting, and Charlie lived with his uncle Albert in their home south of the present Mrs. Mildred Telgard residence.

One evening Charlie was asked by his uncle Albert if he would go out to his feeding bed at the Parmlee place (now Oscar Kitchen's) to bait the traps. There had been rumors of bears and the big bear trap had been set on the pigeon bed. Evening was approaching and there was much heavy woods and very little road. In fact, there were bars across the road at the present Will Steele and Baumberger farms, and from there on no road at all.

Charlie, feeling not quite so brave inwardly as he made himself appear outwardly started out on his favorite pony. The sack of grain was so divided that part of the weight was on each side of the horse's back. As he got out on the lonely road it took every ounce of his courage for the big woods looked dark and menacing. The pony did his best for Charlie didn't bother to stop and open any bars, so over the top they went! Even to the fence around the feeding bed.

But when he got that far, how to scatter the grain? He stopped to think but a minute and then decided to scatter it while still sitting in the saddle. This made it necessary for the horse to walk back and forth over the soft bed. And Charlie lost no time in getting home.

Next day Uncle Albert went over himself. Noting that the bed had been badly tramped over, he muttered to himself about the audacity and carelessness of people, etc. Charlie said never a word at the time. But years afterwards he visited his uncle, then living in Charlevoix, and they were reminiscing over early days and Charlie told him the whole story. Uncle Albert said he had his suspicions but had he known he was afraid he would never have asked him to go.

Many are the tales that could be told about the wild pigeons here at this time and the hunters who came to this vicinity for this sport. The millions of birds here, then within a year, almost none at all.

An article in the Scientific America, some years ago, gives as a possible reason, that the birds, in seeking new feeding places free from the persecution of the hunter, struck out across the ocean and perished from hunger and fatigue.

The National Geographic Magazine (Oct. 1936) has an interesting comment in its articles, "Hunted Birds of Field and Wilds", by Maj. Allen Brooks, and "Game Birds of Prairie, Forest and Tundra", by Alexander Whetmore in the same issue.

Here we learn that they were found in the North Eastern

United States in fabulous abundance in the early days of American history (1740) and, that in the days of our pioneer parents, here in Leelanau County, their numbers were legion.

But the strangest thing of all is their sudden disappearance in 1881.

Roney reports one and one-half million birds shipped from Petoskey alone between March 22 and August 12, 1878. Then to find them gone in three years! It is difficult to account for the complete disappearance of such a large number.

The last wild bird, for which there is certain record, was one killed April 1904, and the final end of the species came when the last surviving bird in captivity died in the Zoological Garden in Cincinnati, Ohio, at one p. m. Central Standard Time September 1, 1914. It was mounted and is now on exhibition in the U. S. National Museum in Washington D.C.

Although there have been rumors of people seeing one occasionally, these rumors, where followed up, have proven false. So far as anyone knows today, the passenger pigeon is extinct.

(The Mourning Dove is much like it, but is not the same, altho' often taken for a wild pigeon.)

By M. S. G.
January 22, 1937

County Officers as per Tribune Oct. 6th 1877.

Sheriff,   George T. Carr.
Under Sheriff,   E. E. Chase.
Deputy   "   ,   Wm. M. Smith.
Clerk,   George Ray.
Deputy Clerk,   S. J. Hutchinson.
Register,   Alfred John.
Prosecuting Atty.,   B. H. Derby.
Circuit Court Comm.,   George A. Cutler.
Treasurer,   William Gill.
Judge of Probate,   C. W. Williams.
Surveyor,   Kasson Freeman.
Coroners,   George N. Smith,   J. E. Fisher.
Alfred John was register in 1882 and
William Hitchcock was Register of Deeds in 1888
according to papers recorded in those years.

Township Treasurers:

1867	H. O. Rose
1868	William Voice.
1871	George L. Lutman
1872	Erastus Bates
1874	Joel W. Ranger
1875	Samuel W. Wilson
1876-77-78	John Kehl
1879	Joshua S. Middleton
1880	George N. Smith
1881-82	Norman C. Morgan
1883	Soloman Steele
1884	Norman C. Morgan
1885-86	Oscar E. Wilbur
1888	George N. Smith

A few early dates

1849 — Waukazooville laid out by Rev. G. N. Smith
1852 — Northport laid out by Deacon Joseph Dame
1850 — Log school house built by Smith and McLaughlin on the shore East of William Gill residence

    1855 — Northport organized into a school district being the first regular public school in county.

    1856 — Small one story frame building erected on present site.

    1867 — Two story upright attached to this making three rooms.

1859 — Log school house built at Bight.
1851 — Grand Traverse County organized, which included Benzie and Leelanau.
1853 — Benzie and Leelanau constitute a township of this county with Samuel W. Boice (Boyce) supervisor.
1855 — Post office established with A. B. Page as postmaster.
                     Succeeded by J. M Burbeck
                             Rev. S. Steele
                             William Gill
                             Howard Gill
                             C. I Wrisley
                             Eva A. Wurzburg

1849 — Rev. G. N. Smith preached
1863 — Congregational society organized (fourteen members.)
1869 — Building started.
1870 — Building completed.
1858 — Methodist class organized.
1859 — Rev. S. Steele made presiding elder.
1869 — Small building erected - Rev. Mathias pastor.
1871 — Corner stone of present building laid. Rev. Deitz pastor in completed building.
1860 — Good Temple Lodge instituted (Feb. 18)
1869 — Masonic Lodge instituted (March 5)
1860 — Traverse Bay Hotel built by Deacon Dame.
1869 —   "   "   "   rented by W. H. Franklin
1871 —   "   "   "   purchased by W. N. Franklin
            "   "   "   purchased by R. A. Campbell

         Now called The Waukazoo.

About 1860 Government men made coast survey, camped in vicinity of Telgard boat establishment, marks or stations made every ½ mile. Traveled by boat and didn't need roads.

1874 — Lutheran church organized.
1876 — Rev. A. Rystad resident pastor.
1886 — Building erected.

Reminiscences

In the early fifties Nicodemus Pickard of Buffalo, New York, organized the company of Pickard and Munger. They purchased a large tract of timber land on North Manitou Island, built the first wood dock in Northern Michigan and a store, thus equiping themselves to supply the ever increasing steamboat demand for cordwood.

It was through the acquaintance with Mr. Pickard that my father, a steamboat captain, came to Michigan. Pickard had also bought a section of land at the Bight where he had built a frame residence, a store, blacksmith shop and boarding house, placing his brother Simeon Pickard and brother-in-law, Walter Barton, in charge. They were soon succeeded by Daniel Buss.

Otis White also built a dock at the Bight at this time (1854) as well as a large log living house, frame barn, small store and blacksmith shop.

My memory of the blacksmith shop is vivid as ox teams were used to haul wood. They were driven into a large trap frame, their legs bound tightly to be shod. The shoes were in two pieces to fit the divided hoof.

The first squatters in the township were located near the Bight. These first settlers were: O. L. White, the Hazel family, John and Andrew Scott, Mr. Vaughn, Mr. Lakes, N. L. and Morris White, Joshua Middleton, John Kehl, John Howell, Wm. Nash, Chauncey Woolsey, Wm. Mitchell, Jack Middleton, H. Hagen, Thos. Retford, Joel Ranger, Buck Brown, Edwin Taylor, William Thomas, Peter and Charles Gustaff, James Emerson, James Martin, William Sprague, Mr. Cole, Mr. Charter,-- All these families being settlers before the Civil War.

A log school house was built in the fall of 1858 on the beach just east of the McNamee cottage and served the district until 1880 when the frame building was built on the hill and used until the consolidation of the schools of Leelanau township. This building was then sold to Orville Kellogg who moved and rebuilt it into the dwelling he now occupies.

The school house at the Bight became the social center of this self-contained community. Here Rev. G. N. Smith held evening services every three weeks in winter. A literary society was organized and lecture courses popularly supported. Spelling matches were common past times, too.

In the fall of 1860, through miscalculation on storms, the winter supply for Pickard and Barton's store was landed at Pickard's dock on Manitou Island. By Christmas time a food shortage looked so serious that Chauncey Woolsey, veteran sailor, volunteered with his 18 ft. sloop-rigged open boat to make the trip to the Island.

They reached the Island safely but the weather looked so doubtful that they took on the cargo in haste and struck out. A winter blizzard with snow and heavy sea came down upon them, the spray freezing where it struck. Moses Dexter was Mr. Woolsey's helper. He despaired of ever reaching the Bight and began to pray and implored the skipper to turn back to the Island. He received scant sympathy and was told to stop praying and bail water and ice out of the boat.

They finally made Cat Head Bay where they literally washed upon the beach. Fortunately, the skippers' brother, Frances Woolsey, one of the first squatters at Cat Head Bay, had a snug cabin here which probably saved their lives. The boat and provisions were later salvaged and brought to the Bight.

By spring, all eatable provisions at the store were consumed, but with game and the vegetables they had, the squatters managed to hold out until navigation again opened.

An early surprise

The summer I was fifteen (1865) I drove an ox team for Dan Buss and had a room at his boarding house at the Bight.

Often passengers from the steam boats coming or going waited for boats to come or go. As no accommodations were provided for guests, I occasionally had a transient bed fellow. One fellow I had occasion to remember as the boat came in during the night. When I dressed the next morning I found some very useful articles of clothing missing. The boat had come and gone!

Some time after this a boat came in from Chicago. A passenger got off, came to the boarding house for the night.

Not to be out done this time I put my clothes under my pillow. I didn't miss a thing!

Next morning I was told that my bed fellow that night had been Perry Hannah of Traverse City waiting for his bay boat, "The Sunnyside" to make his home.

Cattle Thieves

In the latter part of the '60's cattle thieves were operating in the southern part of the county. Valentine Lee was sheriff. He arrested two men--Marvin and Decker. They were lodged in the county jail at Northport. George Dame and Wallace Woolsey were deputy sheriffs to take charge of them.

The prisoners planned an escape which was carried out this way: After quietly submitting to their jail conditions for some time, as the two deputies came in with their dinners on big platters, they dashed against them, slipped out of the door, turned the key and had their two keepers imprisoned. They made for the bush and were never apprehended.

Later they returned to the southern part of the county where they made their homes.

From Byron Woolsey
1936

OUR EARLY SCHOOLS

Our first white settlers of importance being a missionary, of course schools were of second importance, but he also had a family of young children, so our first school was school on week days and church on Sundays.

It was located on what is Main Street now about half way between Waukazoo Street and the Railroad on the south side of the Street.

This was built in 1850.

There were many private schools in the early days and some of the teachers were: Miss Emmeline Wood, Miss Amanda Randall, Libby Ingalls, Miss Holcomb (who afterwards was Mrs. Ed Vannakenbury) Anna John, Voila John, Mr. Severence, and Miss Norton, later Mrs. Massa.

There were two Government Schools in this township. The New Mission School at Omena and Onomineese on Lake Michigan, just west of the Alfred Johnson farm home. The buildings are gone now, but the cemetery is still in use.

One of the early teachers was Mrs. Jessie Morgan, mother of Norman Morgan. Mr. and Mrs. Joel Ranger, and Miss Esther Ranger also taught there.

In 1855, Northport was organized into a school district under the common school law, being the first regular public school organized within the present limits of Leelanau County. This school still remains District No. I of Leelanau Township.

In 1856, a small one-story frame building was erected on the sight of the present school building and of which, is still a part, if only a coal-bin.

In 1867, a two-story upright was attached to the school building, this brought our school up to a three-room school.

About 1890, two more rooms were added on the south side.

In 1910, what is now the north part of our school was built and then in 1921, the six districts out of 7 of Leelanau Township were consolidated into Leelanau Township Consolidated School District No. I.

Before 1880 as our tale is supposed to be told, we had a district school at Omena, Craker district, (south of town) the Bight, and the Light house. These were the names of the different schools.

Many tales are told of these early schools and their teachers. The teachers had all grades and sizes of pupils, from tots to grown men and girls.

THE BIGHT SCHOOL

The old log school house at the Bight was built in 1859. Afterwards it was replaced by a nice frame building.

Some of the early teachers were Miss Lida Chapin, Almon Ingalls and Elizabeth Ingalls. The Ingalls lived at Ingall's Bay near Omena. The Bay was named for that family.

The story goes that while Miss Ingalls taught at the Bight School, she took all her brothers and sisters with her each day to school at the Bight and that there were seven in all.

Then followed Eben Decow, Miss Lindley (later Mrs. Mebert) Mrs. Chapin, Miss Voice (later Mrs. Wilber Steele), Miss Clara Wrisley, William J. Woolsey, and Mrs. A. W. Hall. Her descendants are still with us and she was a cousin of Stephan A. Douglass, whose name was often in history, during the Civil War days.

Several other teachers' names have been handed but not the dates. These were Miss Harriet Middleton (later Mrs. Geo. Craker), Mr. Parmelee, Mr. Leax and Miss Sarah Budd (later Mrs. Ed. Kemp).

THE NEW MISSION SCHOOL

The New Mission School was moved in the spring of 1852 from Old Mission on the Peninsula to Omena, under the supervision of Rev. Peter Dougherty.

The pupils were limited to 50--25 boys and 25 girls. Here the boys learned farming and shop work, under the direction of Mrs. Geo A. Craker, John Porter. Some of their descendants are still with us in this township.

The girls learned housework and sewing. All had religious training.

Some of the early teachers were Miss Isabella Morrison of New Haven, Conn., Miss Catherine Gibson of Pennsylvania, Miss Beach, Mr. John Porter, Miss Hennrietta Dougherty from Pa. and New York.

This school continued until the Civil War, when it was hard to get funds. Then the property passed to other hands.

OMENA SCHOOLS
Contributed By W. A. Craker   Omena, Mich.

The first school that I have any remembrance of was held in the old S. Kimmerhorn house, which stood close to the shore and just north a short distance from the present home of Mrs. N. C. Morgan. Miss Louisa Woolsey taught. I can just remember being there a visitor.

Later school was held in a room in the house of Mr. B. F. Holcomb. I am unable to name the teacher, but I can remember being there just slightly. Perhaps it was Miss Woolsey.

After this, school was kept in a log house owned by Wm. Milson. Mr. Milson was the teacher. Then in 1869 school was again kept in the old Milson house and Miss Cornelia Dougherty was the teacher and I attended as a very little boy.

The first school in Omena that I remember about and which I attended for the first time was in the Dougherty house (now known as the Omena Inn).

Miss Louise Dougherty was the teacher. This was in 1868.

School was held later in the Memigona house and Henry Dougherty was teacher.

The Omena School house was not built until long after the one in the Craker District. I can't tell you just what year. It just seems to me there was an interval of time when school was not carried on.

Among the teachers who taught in this school were Miss Smith, Miss Minerva Bigelow, Miss Myrtie Rose, Miss Anna Hillard, Miss Jessie Wolf, and Miss Dorland.

The Omena School house is now used as a garage on the farm of Delbert Joynt.

CRAKER SCHOOL
Contributed by W. A. Craker   Omena, Mich.,

In the year 1870, what is known as the Craker School house was built. Before this there was no regular school house in this District No. 5.

Miss Harriet Porter was the first teacher. Miss Cornelia Dougherty was next, then Miss Samantha Keyes, Miss Cameron, Miss Barnhardt, Miss Elizabeth Chase, Mr. Frank Holcomb and Miss Minerva Bigelow. Then Fred Green and that takes us up to 1880.

The Craker school house is still standing on the original site, but has been converted into a farm home by Earl Brown.

LIGHT HOUSE SCHOOL

I have been unable to get any information on the Light House School so far, but I have not given up trying.

Respectfully submitted
Alice Gill Scott

Mr. Woolsey also tells us of a sleigh ride that was enjoyed by the children of the Bight school in 1859.

Francis Woolsey took the children and young people with him to Onominese to visit the Indian school there. Mrs. Morgan was the teacher and it was quite a village at the time. Also, it was a considerable journey at that time. The Indians must have appreciated the visit for they returned the call, coming with their ponies and all their regalia--feathers, moccasins and all.

EARLY TEACHERS
Contributed by Norman Thomas

The first School Commissioner was Mrs. A. B. Dunlap. The second was S. G. Hutchinson and the third was E. J. Dinsmore.

Some of the early teachers, probably mostly in private schools were:

Emeline Wood, Amanda Randall, Libby Ingalls, Miss Halcomb (later Mrs. Ed Vanvalkenberg) Anna John (Mrs. Ed Charter), Viola John (Mrs. Clifford Barns, Harbor Springs) and Mr. Severence.

From 1856 to 1862 there were no teachers assigned. Oscar Wilblur thinks E. Cromwell Tuttle taught the term in the winter of 62 - 63---the year he says the first little school house was built on the site of the present school premises.

Then he places O. C. Moffatt from 1865 to 1867 and then A. P. Gray and Leo Stacey who was once a county official while the county seat was at Northport.

The following are the teachers according to the years:

1870 - 1871 -- William Woolsey, Louise Woolsey.
1871 - 1872 -- Nettie Braman, Clara Wrisley.
1872 - 1873 -- Albert Saylor, Clara Hill (?)
1873 - 1874 -- E. O. Brown (Fall '73 started-Pettitt finished) Thomas Pettitt, Clara Hill
1874 - 1875 -- Thomas Pettitt, Cornelia Dougherty
1875 - 1876 -- Amorette Fisk Hall, Hattie Parmelee
1876 - 1877 -- Thomas Pettitt, Ella Saurs, W. J. Pettitt
1877 - 1878 -- Thomas B. Pettitt, Emma Barnard
1878 - 1879 -- W. J. Cox (?)
1879 - 1880 -- P. D. Cornell
1880 - 1881 -- May Cornell
1881 - 1882 -- May Cornell
1882 - 1883 -- May Cornell (with Cora White filling out in the lower grades)
1883 - 1884 -- Samuel Warwick, Mrs. Warwick, Miss Anna Hillard
1884 - 1885 -- Wm. Jones, Mrs. Jones, Bertha Bushee
1885 - 1886 -- Elizabeth Dorland - Buckworth, Miss Myrtle Rose, Della Dorland - Craker
1886 - 1887 -- E. E. Rogers (Scholars Mutined) Miss Myrta Rose (?)
1887 - 1888 -- Eva Smith, Mina Fletcher, Dinnie Fletcher
1888 - 1889 -- Eva Smith Franklin, Jennie Grant, Amelia Miller
1889 - 1890 -- Chas. P. Savage, Mary Blacken, Jennie Grant
1890 - 1891 -- M. A. McKeever, Jennie Grant, Margret Anderson
1891 - 1892 -- E. J. Peck, Margret Anderson, Jessie Wolf - Hilton
1892 - 1893 -- A. E. Dinsmore (Died Feb. 6, 1893) S. R. Burke, Mable Butters, Carrie Bartlett, Maggie Anderson
1893 - 1894 -- Ward Tower, Ella Leslie, Julia Miller Maggie Anderson
1894 - 1895 -- Ward Tower, Ella Leslie, Miss Anderson

(part of the year), Miss Morton (finished year) Eddie Primeau
1895 - 1896 -- Wm. Russell, Nellie Erickson, Florence
L. Bragdon.

MEN IN THE UNION ARMY

It is hard for us to realize that Northport was almost as large, numerically, in 1860-70 as it is now. Let us look at the number who enlisted for service in the Civil War.

One group left Northport for Traverse City January 1864 by team--but the road was so difficult and perhaps the horses not the best, that often they had to help the horses instead of the horses aiding them. So, when they reached Traverse City they sent the team back and started out afoot. It took them ten days to reach Grand Rapids where they were mustered into service. Near Muskegon, however, they hired a team to take them into Grand Rapids and this cost them fifty dollars.

There were six men in this group--Chauncey Woolsey, the oldest, was forty-eight years old and was killed the following May 30 in a skirmish just after Grants' drive in the Wilderness. The others were: John Kehl, Joshia Middleton, (wounded in wrist) Thomas Haynes, Charles Waltz, (wounded in leg) and Thomas McCormick.

Edmund P. Taylor volunteered and served three years and two months. He returned and took a homestead at Cat Head.

Others who served in the Union Army were: John Thomas, Payson Wolfe, Wallace Woolsey, Francis Woolsey (sons of Chauncey Woolsey) William Voice, Henry Budd, Edgar Taylor, Henry Holcomb, William Hickox, John Scott, Andrew Scott, John Howell, Edgar Charter, Wallace McClellan, Philip Easternight, Albert Powers, Edward VanValtenberg, James Martin, Jesse Morgan (died).

AN HISTORIC BIBLE

Rev. George N. Smith, first white settler and first pastor and organizer of the Congregational Church, presented Captain Chauncey Woolsey with a Bible. Mr. Woolsey was one of the first deacons of the church. This Bible was given to Capt. Woolsey on his departure for the Civil War. He was then 48 years old and the senior member in the group of recruits before mentioned, who left Northport January 1864. Capt. Woolsey was killed in Grant's drive in the Wilderness May 30, 1864 and this Bible was returned to his son Byron woolsey.

When his son Clinton left for service in the World War the same Bible was presented to him. After his tragic death in the Aviation service in Buenos Aires May 21, 1930, it was returned to his father Byron Woolsey, then eighty years old.

January 1936
Contributed by Byron Woolsey

The following article has been taken from the diary of
Joshua S.Middleton,of Northport:

I left home Thursday at 4 a.m..At noon left Northport
for Suttons Bay.Others in the group of recruits included;
Chauncey Woolsey,the oldest, John Kehl, Charles Waltz, and
Thomas McCormick. We arrived in Suttons Bay the same day.We
arrived in Traverse City Friday night,cold and hungry.Snow
had been three feet deep with much of the road not having been
broken most of the way.From Traverse we hired a team of horses,
but which through our haste proved only worthy of carrying our
baggage. The teamster turned back within five miles of Benzonia,and it was snowing,cold and dissagreable. We managed to
find a place to stay over night in a new settlers home. They
were very nice folk,with the women folk taking a great fancy
to some cheese we had,in our meager supplies. But we dared not
refuse them for fear of the consequences. It turned out that
they charged a very reasonable price for our stay.They wished
us well.
 Monday; We ate our dinner in a woods on the way,a cloudy day.
We kept going until nightfall when we realized we had taken the
wrong road. Having to turn back,we were so very tired and lame,
our minds were about to made up to go back home. We instead
kept on, and when most discouraged managed to find the right
guide marker of our route. We slept over night with(Smith's)
in their small log house,with no bed. We had very little extra
clothing with which to cover us, and were so cold we could not
sleep at all. We did have plenty to eat,though we paid high for
it. John Kehl had told the women that I had fourteen children
that there was only one inch height difference in their size,
from the oldest to the youngest,and in standing them in a row
was looking like a line of steps!

We reached Manistee at 4P.M. the next day. Started for
Lincoln in the morning,arriving the next night. We were so sore
footed and stiff,it seemed as if we could not move on any furthe
Tom Haines,suffered the worse.The next morning we got a team
for which we paid $50.00 to take us on further. This took about
all we had, but it would not have been cheaper to stay. We made
Pentwater the next night,but could not stay over,and traveled
on til morning until we reached Muskegon. Then at Perrysburg
we took train to Grand Rapids, having had no sleep or anthing
to eat since leaving Pentwater. We arrived before dinner, the
23rd of January,1864,

Feb.8,1864
We came through on the Detroit and Milwaukee Railroad to
Detroit,Toledo,Pittsburg,Little York, arriving at Harrisburg,Pa.
about sundown.In Baltimore we had our breakfast, and arrived at
Washington. Here we received our equipment. We are near Dixie.
We stayed here two days, then it was off to the front. First
Brandy Station, then off to our camp. We built us a little
cabin and began to be soldiers, doing picket duty through the
winter on the Rappahanock.

We have been assigned to the 26th Michigan Volunteers,Compa
A..Here we also found Henry Holcomb of Northport.

Constitution and By-Laws
of
Woolsey Post No. 399, Grand Army of the Republic
Department of Mich.

The Common Parliamentary Code of the State of Michigan shall apply in all proceedings, not otherwise provided for.

Permanent officers to be voted for and then approved by the Commander.

The Commander shall fill temorary vacancy of any office, at any meeting

Meetings are to be cohtinued and held from time to time according to a majority vote of each meeting.

Meetings may be called(at any time) by the Commander on giving suitable notice.

Any proceedings and necessary business may be voted upon and tr - ansacted by those present - at any meeting, with previous notice. If neither Commander, 1st V.·., or Vice Commander be present at a regular appointed meeting, a Commander may be appointed-pro tem- by those present.

The Election Laws of the State shall apply to the election and qualification' of officers of this Post.

The Rules and Regulations of the National G.A.R. shall apply to this Post- without imbodied in these By-Laws.

By - Laws of this Post may be added to or changed at any time by a vote of 2/3 of the members present, at any properly notified or appointed meeting for sais purpose.

This Post shall be constituted a Relief Post, and each Comrade shall contribute annually $1.00. To be paid to the quartermaster in quarterly installments of 25¢. to form a Relief Fund.

Executive Business Committees of three trustees whaose duty shall be to transact all business not otherwise provided for to be elected by the Post, and approved by the Commander.

A Finance Committee of three are to examine and report on all expenditures of money, bills, claims, and accounts as recorded by the Quartermaster and Adjutant.

Northport, was dedicated to his memory.

The Woolsey Post No.399, Grand Army of the Republic, Department of Michigan, was named for Chauncey Woolsey, Captain, killed in the Civil War.

Other Northport Men who Served in the Union Army , include; Edmund P. Taylor, John Thomas, Payson Wolfe, Wallace Woolsey and Francis Woolsey (both sons of Chauncy Woolsey), William Voice, Henry Budd, Edgar Taylor, Henry Holcomb (killed in action), William Hickox, John Scott, Andrew Scott, John Howell, Edgar Charter, Wallace McClellan, Philip Easternight, Albert Powers, Edmund Van Valtenburg, James Martin, Jesse Morgan (who died in service).